W9-DAE-418

# THE COMPLETE GUIDE TO
# STA ORMATS

## TAPED FORMATS FOR TELEVISION

# THE COMPLETE GUIDE TO STANDARD SCRIPT FORMATS

## PART II - TAPED FORMATS FOR TELEVISION

Compiled and written by

Judith H. Haag

© CMC PUBLISHING
11642 Otsego Street
North Hollywood, California 91601

Printed in the United States of America.

---

For information write CMC Publishing, 11642 Otsego Street,
North Hollywood, California 91601

---

Revised June, 1988, Judith H. Haag
Third printing March, 1994

---

Cover design by George E. Johannesson, Jr., North Hollywood,
California

---

ISBN 0-929583-01-9

---

WITH GRATEFUL ACKNOWLEDGMENT TO...


Lyle Law whose script format knowledge and expertise made this manual possible.

Lyle has been lending credibility to movie and television scripts for over fifteen years.  As a Format Specialist he has served in the positions of head script typist at CMC Script Service and as Supervisor of the Script Department at CBS.



... and special thanks to Bert Guillen who's been in the script business forever and who willingly lent his valuable expertise.



... and heartfelt gratitude to Marilyn Wright who knows more about scripts (and most other things) than practically anyone else, and who encouraged, inspired, prodded, supported and assisted the rewriting, editing and polishing of this volume... and then spent a million hours in front of the word processor typing and formatting it.

## FOREWORD

The following information and advice
should prove helpful whether
you are contemplating writing a
television script or have already
written several.

## THERE'S NO BUSINESS LIKE SHOW BUSINESS

So you've watched TV and thought to yourself:

"I can write that stuff."

Here's what to do:

### WRITE A SPEC SCRIPT:

"Writing on spec" means nobody asked you to do it and chances are nobody will pay for it when it's done. What a spec script is for, is a sample of your writing. With it, someone will invite you to "pitch"* for their show.

About your spec script... miracles being what they are, you might... it's possible... you could sell it. But miracles are beyond the scope of this book. Let's just say that the requirement of your script is A) to learn how to, and B) to get it read.

First B).

### HOW TO GET YOUR SCRIPT READ:

Upon every producer's desk sets a slush pile. This is where your finished script will wait. The producer will thumb through the slush pile for interesting reading. Your script has to look the part. If it's too short, too long, too wordy, too anything, he won't take it to the bathroom with him.

So that is the goal of this book; to enable you to type the form right so the producer will take your script to the bathroom. Also, when you type your script in the right form it will help you to think in the right form and it <u>will</u> be a script.

Many new writers feel, "Write a script?... nothing to it; put it in the right form?... Oh, no!!!" This book will take the fear out of scriptwriting. This book is the state of the art in tab setting.

Now. Pick a show. Your favorite.

### IS IT FILM OR TAPE? AND HERE'S THE DIFFERENCE:

In film you can have two characters... jogging... on a yacht... attacked by enemy helicopters.

In tape you have them sitting at the kitchen table.

Generally, film goes anywhere; tape stays in the studio, with few sets.

Tape is more like a play than it is like a movie. Rethink car chases... there is less action, more reaction.

If you want to write a film show such as "Magnum P.I." or even "Little House of the Prairie", then get the first book in this series, <u>THE COMPLETE GUIDE TO STANDARD SCRIPT FORMATS - PART I</u>. It's terrific. It will tell you everything you'll need to know about format for moviemaking and film for TV

P.S. M.A.S.H. is a film show, not tape. It uses one camera film technique. It's covered in Part I. If you want to write teleplay, this is the book to use.

*pitch -- to "take a meeting"- with story editors and/or producer of a show wherein you razzle dazzle them with possible story areas. They might want one. You will get a "go-ahead". This means money so, go ahead.

## HOW TO WRITE A SITUATION COMEDY:

Study the show you've chosen.

Know the characters... the rhythm of their words; how they react and interact. What are the sets? Use them, don't invent others. Who are the people? Have the stories be theirs. Use an outside character only as a catalyst.

Is the show physical (LaVerne and Shirley), or issue oriented (Barney Miller). A story suited to one would be handled differently on the other.

Once you feel you really know the show, decide on a story.

## WHERE IDEAS COME FROM:

-- Think of the characters... in what situation would you like to see them? (George Jefferson suddenly broke.) What situations would be likely? (Middle-age and middle-class might also mean middle minded. Have the character take up exercise. Is there a story there?)

-- Scan TV Guide" -- read the loglines for all the shows, even cartoons and especially the 3 a.m. movies.

-- Also, read the newspapers. There are a million stories in the naked city.

-- But mostly, look to yourself -- everything there is to know about Every-man is within every man.

Once you start to brainstorm, there is no stopping the onslaught of ideas. However, ideas are the only thing inflation hasn't hit. They're still a dime a dozen.

It's what you do with your ideas that give them value.

## WHAT IS STORY:

Story is what happens to the characters. It is a complete thought with beginning, middle, and end. Be able to say your story out loud in a few sentences.

Before you've gotten this far you possibly already have a show in mind and the story you want to tell.

## ON TO STRUCTURE:

A sitcom is the last two acts of a three act play. Since we already know the characters, we don't have to be introduced to them; we can get right to what happens, and what happens has to start on page three. (If you get a phone call from a vague acquaintance and he asks, "How are you? How's your dog?", you're going to be more or less uneasy until he gets to the point. That's what you have to get to by page three... the point. By the act break you have to get to the crisis that's going to be so enrapturing we'll want to wait through the commercials to see what happens next.

So, Act One -- chase him up a tree. Act Two -- have him try every which way to get down out of the tree and get down finally, solved and resolved.

In a screenplay you can develop your people. They are changed. In situation comedy the situation changes, the people stay the same. That way we will tune in week after week to see how our old friends will surprise and delight us with further hijinx.

When you have your idea, and how you're going to unravel it:

## DO AN OUTLINE

Ask yourself, what has to happen in this scene... and then what... and then what. Write in short notes. Do not be elaborate. It's just map to get you where you're going. Any holes or changes are a lot easier to fix in the outline than in the script. Now you know exactly what you're going to write.

## READY... BEGIN:

Watch the episode that's playing out in your head and put it on the paper.

Now what.

## HOW TO GET AN AGENT:

... Any way you can. Here is where the real creativity comes in. Send it to his mother. Have your third cousin who used to be a caddy for Jerry Vale, get you a personal reference. Also, you might want to write to the Writer's Guild:

> 8955 Beverly Blvd.
> Los Angeles, CA 90048

For a nominal fee, they will send you a list of accredited agents. Get the list. Send your material. You will get it back unopened. It will break your heart. Sent it out again.

An agent will not get you work. (Ask anybody who has one.) What you are after is a partnership. You supply terrific material -- he will hustle meetings. You get terrific response at meetings -- he draws up the contracts. Agent or not -- go everywhere, see everyone; but don't even bother until you have a well-written script.

## CAN I SUCCEED IN HOLLYWOOD, IF I LIVE IN PADUCAH:

Well, there's always stamps.

Besides, something happens. Because you're not here; you're not jaded. When you look at a show on the air, you just see the show and not the goobleygook that might be behind it. That gives you a chance at clear vision. You have the opportunity to come up with the one fresh idea the staff would love to hear.

However, if you do move to Hollywood... Warning: This will take a minute so go ahead and unpack the U-Haul.

## STEALING

Everyone thinks his idea is unique; that his script is special and that everyone else is out to steal it. This is true. Your script is special; your idea is unique. It will be stolen. Not because anybody will see it; but because it will just come out of another typewriter across the state. It's the collective unconscious and it happens all the time.

(If it makes you feel better, send a copy of your script to yourself registered mail or register it at the Writer's Guild.)

## POSTSCRIPT:

So now you have endured all the heebie jeebies, gone through fourteen drafts, your wife won't even consider a reconciliation, and your dog still growls at you... okay, okay, but you have a finished script. You tune in the show one last time and there... there is your story. They are doing your story!!! And they are doing it all wrong!!!

Welcome to Hollywood.

                                                          Viki King

# BIOGRAPHIES

Judith H. Haag

B.S. Degree, Communications, Southern Illinois University
Teacher, high school English and speech
Writing Consultant, Educational Film Strip Series for BFA
General Manager, CMC Script Service
Supervisor, Barbara's Place Script Service,
  West Hollywood, California



Viki King

B.S. Degree, Communications, Southern Illinois University
Writer, network television since 1969
Studio engineer. NBC Burbank, Tonight Show
Consultant to the BBC in Children's Programming
Writer/Producer, National Educational Television
Lecturer, UCLA (in scriptwriting)
Script Consultant
Member of Writers Guild of America
Author of <u>How to Write a Movie in 21 Days</u>, Harper & Row 1988

Available as guest lecturer and script consultant.  For further
information write:  Viki King, P.O. Box 563, Malibu, CA 90265

# TABLE OF CONTENTS

## TAPE-LIVE FORMAT

| Page | CONTENTS |
|---|---|

| Page | CONTENTS |
|------|----------|

**VARIETY, AWARD AND SPECIAL SHOWS**

| Page | CONTENTS |
|---|---|

## SOME WORDS ABOUT THE IMPORTANCE OF SCRIPTS AND SCRIPT FORMATS

The script is the basic tool of the movie and television industry. No script, no show. No matter how spontaneous a television show or film may seem, you can be absolutely sure that there was a script involved. Scripts are used for everything from game shows to talk shows to charity telethons to documentaries.

And so, important as it is that there be a script, equally important is the necessity for that script to be written in the correct standard format appropriate for a given filming situation. A one camera feature film production requires a specific script format quite different from a taped television production.

The standard script formats which are universally used in the movie and television industry today have evolved because each one is designed to suit a specific filming situation. Therefore, script formats are not just randomly spaced words scattered on a page. Each script format is logically and concisely planned to accommodate the unique aspects of a particular filming situation. One can well imagine that it would be utterly impossible to gather up a novel and a camera, go out on location, and shoot a film. The book must be re-written -- translated if you will -- into a film format script. No easy job, as is attested to by the fact that those who are talented at this formidable task receive Academy Awards for screen adaptations!

Since formats vary to accommodate a specific filming circumstance, it is by the same token true that one cannot make a film format into a taped television format merely by changing the spacing and re-setting the typewriter tabs. Film formats and television formats are not interchangeable. Translating from one format to another requires a (frequently major) re-write of the entire script. (See Format Comparison Chart, Page 4)

There are many reasons for strictly adhering to a consistent standard format. A given script must serve as a basic tool which is used by many hands -- directors, technicians, actors, and many others. It must serve as a handle which each can easily catch hold of to facilitate that filming endeavor. The right tool must be used for the right job.

Not only does a standard format provide a framework and essential guideline for a specific filming technique, it also serves as an indicator for timings. One script page in proper format generates approximately one minute of "screen time". A taped show page may, however, be less than a minute of screen time since the page a minute formula varies more in taped formats.

Standard script formats, though, involve much more than typewriter tab settings and correct spacings; hence the necessity for a guide such as this. What follows in these pages are the nuts and bolts of taped formats.

## HOW TO USE THIS MANUAL

This book does not belong strictly to the liberal arts. It does not teach creative writing. It is more suited to the manual arts, for it is a book about form and the rules that apply to that form. The form is called a script. This book will show you how to form your creative ideas into a standard script form. It will teach you how to build a script. Like poetry formats, script formats must be mastered completely so as not to restrict the art but to make it fulfill its intended purpose.

So, this is a manual, a how-to-do-it book with many uses. It is designed to be used as a text for the classroom. A person familiar with format can use it as an easy reference for format details. For others, it can be a self-teaching tool. Quick reference sheets to keep at your typewriter, a glossary, and an index -- all make this book suitable to many needs.

The completed manual, in two parts, will cover four formats: Film, Tape-Live, Three-Camera, and Tape-Live for Variety, Award and Special shows. Revisions, shooting and taping schedules, rehearsal schedules, short and long rundowns are included as a part of these basic formats.

At this point it is extremely important that you take time to read through the table of contents, keeping the following in mind. If you were to pick up a script and start reading, the cover would be first, then the fly page, then the first page of the script. Note that the table of contents is ordered in the same way. Continuing then with the script, you would read the first page heading, the opening scene heading, some stage direction, a character's cue, dialogue and so on. The contents follow that same order.

Now read through the contents.

The contents give you a good idea of the material. Now notice the layout of the text itself by flipping through the pages. With few exceptions, all exposition is on the left; all examples illustrating the text are on the right. Examples are mostly placed at the correct tab settings with a Courier 72, 10 pitch IBM element in order that you may become accustomed to seeing the various parts of the script properly placed on the page. Hopefully, this visualizing will assist you greatly in learning for, like poetry, scripts are visual forms with content.

## WHAT ARE TAPED SHOWS?

There are two basic script formats: filmed formats used for "movies" and taped formats used for many television shows. Filmed format, also called one camera format, is covered in Part I of THE COMPLETE GUIDE TO STANDARD SCRIPT FORMATS. Taped format is the subject of this volume.

Because "taping" is totally different from "filming," it follows that the script formats are inherently different also. The major difference between these two mediums is that filming takes place mainly on location, whereas taping takes place in a studio before a live audience. Taping utilizes a three-camera technique originally developed by Desi Arnaz and cameraman, Karl Freund, in the taping of "I Love Lucy." Hence, the origin of the term three-camera.

It is important to note that several terms are used to refer to video taped shows. The term "three-camera" is used even though five or more television cameras may be used in the actual taping of a "three-camera" show. The term "television show" seems to contrast taped format with the format used in movies. However, it can also mislead since many television shows are filmed rather than taped! Sitcom (situation comedy) is also used to refer to taped shows. All these terms tend to be used interchangeably. The term taped will be used here.

Taped shows... sitcoms, variety shows, soap operas, game shows, etc., are shot on video tape in a television studio. By necessity these shows are taped in segmented fashion to allow breaks for set changes, commercials, and station breaks. The dress rehearsal is done before a closed audience. Some production companies tape the dress rehearsal and later, edit segments of this taping in the final print. The final taping of the show occurs before a full audience. Depending on re-takes, set changes, costume changes, number of scenes, and any number of other variables, the actual taping time for a half hour taped show may be two or three hours.

Glancing at a page of taped format and then at a page of filmed format reveals easily observable visual differences. A page of taped format contains fewer words and thus more "air." There are fewer set headings. Set headings are shorter and less detailed than filmed scene headings. Dialogue comprises a greater percentage of the script and is double spaced. Stage direction appears capitalized. In short, the visual differences are significant.

Pick up any final script of a taped show and compare it to that of a filmed show. A half hour taped show will probably be under fifty pages. There may be a couple of blue pages spaced through the script to designate commercials and/or station breaks. In the front of some taped scripts you may find a short rundown (a kind of table of contents/timing form), a rehearsal and taping schedule, a cast page, a sets page, and so on. An hour taped variety show may have as many as fifteen "front pages" including all of the above along with pages of staff and crew lists, containing names, addresses, and phone numbers of various show personnel.

The point to be taken here is extremely important: a script is not a script is not a script! Taped format meets the requirements of the specific techniques and tools used in taping a show. Filmed format meets those of filming a show. The techniques and tools for each are different indeed. Taped scripts and filmed scripts are therefore not interchangeable. Technology determines format; therefore, what does change format is change in the technology itself.

Part II of THE COMPLETE GUIDE TO STANDARD SCRIPT FORMATS deals with the two standard formats used in taping for television. Also detailed is the taped format used for variety shows.

Basic differences between Filmed
formats and Taped television formats.

| FILMED FORMAT (Features and action/ location TV Shows) | TAPED FORMAT (Sitcoms, Variety shows, Game shows, Talk shows, etc.) |
|---|---|
| Mainly filmed on locations with the interior scenes shot either on location or in a studio. | Shot exclusively in a studio. Nearly all scenes are interiors. |
| Movie Camera more portable & versatile for location filming. | T.V. Camera more cumbersome & less mobile, but works well on the smooth floor of a studio. |
| Format: Single spaced with double spacing used to separate elements. | Format: Basically double spaced. Single spacing used only in direction. |
| Format: Upper/lower case with only scene headings in all CAPS. | Format: All caps with only dialogue in upper/lower case. |
| Scene Headings: Longer & more detailed, sometimes using camera angles and camera subject, as well as the INT. or EXT. location & time of day. | Scene Headings: Called Set Headings, use only basic information re: INT. and time of day. (EXT. not often used.) |
| Format: Camera & sound cues CAPPED in direction. | Format: Camera cues underlined in direction. Sound cues capped, isolated at margin, underlined. |
| Stage Direction accompanying master scenes is longer, more explanatory and detailed. | Stage Direction brief... usually only a few lines. |
| Dialogue & Direction share job of carrying the story & action. | Dialogue mainly carries the story and action. |
| Characters: Many involved. | Characters: Only a few. In series, regulars appear consistently. |

Two different formats are used in taped scripts.  The first discussed here is one called "Tape-Live" format (sometimes called standard format).  The second is called "Three-Camera" format (sometimes referred to as variation format).

Tape-Live Format...

... is an essentially left-sided format since none of the material extends much past the center of the page.  Both direction and dialogue lines are quite short -- around thirty characters (and spaces) long or approximately 3 inches.

Three-Camera Format...

... is more centered on the page.  The direction extends from margin to margin.  The dialogue is centered with considerable space on each side.

Personal direction appears within the dialogue but is set apart by parentheses and capitalization.  Sets (scene headings) in Three-Camera Format are lettered rather than numbered.

Whether Tape-Live or Three-Camera Format is used depends on the preference of production company personnel.  It is strictly an optional consideration since either is correct and works.  Consistency is the important consideration.

To help visualize the general differences between these two formats, see the following three pages which are examples of a) Tape-Live and b) Three-Camera Formats respectively.

Note:  When writing a spec script for an existing show, it is essential to present the script in the particular format used on the show.

SERIES TITLE

"Episode Title"

ACT ONE

Scene 1


FADE IN:

SET HEADING

(STAGE DIRECTION STAGE DIRECTION
STAGE DIRECTION STAGE DIRECTION)

             CHARACTER

    Dialogue dialogue.  Dialogue

    dialogue... Dialogue, dialogue,

    dialogue dialogue.

(PERSONAL DIRECTION)

             CHARACTER

    Dialogue dialogue.  Dialogue

    dialogue, dialogue dialogue.

(STAGE DIRECTION STAGE DIRECTION,
STAGE DIRECTION STAGE DIRECTION)

             CHARACTER

    Dialogue dialogue dialogue

    dialogue.  Dialogue?  Dialogue.

(PERSONAL DIRECTION PERSONAL

DIRECTION)

             CHARACTER

    Dialogue dialogue?

             CHARACTER

    Dialogue.

<u>SERIES TITLE</u>

"Episode Title"

<u>ACT ONE</u>

<u>A</u>

<u>FADE IN</u>:

<u>SET HEADING</u>
(Cast, Cast, Cast)

STAGE DIRECTION STAGE DIRECTION STAGE DIRECTION.  STAGE
DIRECTION, STAGE DIRECTION STAGE DIRECTION.  STAGE DIRECTION,
STAGE DIRECTION.

CHARACTER CUE

Dialogue dialogue.  Dialogue dialogue...

dialogue?  Dialogue dialogue dialogue

dialogue (PERSONAL DIRECTION) dialogue --

dialogue.

CHARACTER CUE

(PERSONAL DIRECTION)  Dialogue.

Dialogue, dialogue dialogue dialogue.

STAGE DIRECTION STAGE DIRECTION STAGE DIRECTION STAGE
DIRECTION.

CHARACTER CUE

Dialogue dialogue dialogue dialogue.

STAGE DIRECTION STAGE DIRECTION STAGE DIRECTION STAGE
DIRECTION.

CHARACTER CUE

Dialogue dialogue dialogue. (PERSONAL

DIRECTION) Dialogue dialogue dialogue.

CHARACTER CUE

Dialogue dialogue dialogue dialogue.

CHARACTER CUE

Dialogue dialogue dialogue dialogue.

STAGE DIRECTION STAGE DIRECTION STAGE DIRECTION STAGE DIRECTION.

CHARACTER CUE

Dialogue dialogue dialogue.

CHARACTER CUE

(PERSONAL DIRECTION) Dialogue...

dialogue dialogue dialogue dialogue.

CHARACTER CUE

Dialogue... (PERSONAL DIRECTION) ...

dialogue dialogue dialogue dialogue.

STAGE DIRECTION STAGE DIRECTION STAGE DIRECTION STAGE DIRECTION.
STAGE DIRECTION STAGE DIRECTION. STAGE DIRECTION.

CHARACTER CUE

Dialogue dialogue dialogue dialogue.

CHARACTER CUE

Dialogue dialogue dialogue?

CHARACTER CUE

Dialogue dialogue. (PERSONAL DIRECTION)

Dialogue, dialogue dialogue dialogue.

(PERSONAL DIRECTION)

While the look of these two formats is quite different, there are also those elements of information that are handled the same way in both. The similarities and differences listed below will hopefully serve to clarify the overall picture.

## SIMILARITIES IN BOTH FORMATS

1)    Cover and Fly Page

2)    Page Numbers

3)    Acts

4)    FADE IN:

5)    SET HEADINGS (same format and same margin)

6)    General sound cues in direction

7)    Camera cues in direction

8)    Abbreviations in direction (F.G., O.C., B.G.)

9)    SFX:  and SPFX:

10)   (V.O.) and (O.C.) by the character cue

11)   (MORE)

12)   (CONT'D)

## DIFFERENCES BETWEEN BOTH FORMATS

1)    Tab settings and cutoffs

2)    Scenes (lettered in Three-Camera)

3)    Act and scene endings

4)    Personal direction

## DEFINITIONS OF GENERAL TERMS NEEDED
## BEFORE PROCEEDING

**SET HEADING**      A heading which tells where a given scene takes place along with the time of day. (DAY, NIGHT, etc.) It is capitalized, underlined, and isolated at the left margin.

**STAGE DIRECTION**      Information describing setting, situation, character, technical instruction, etc., needed to facilitate the story line.

**CHARACTER CUE**      Personal, short instructions intended for a specific character. These appear capitalized in parentheses at the left margin in Tape-Live Format and appear capitalized in parentheses within the dialogue in Three-Camera Format. Examples: (SITS), (READS LETTER), (PAUSE, REFERS TO PHONE)

**DIALOGUE**      Words spoken by characters. Includes also his "thinking out loud", talking over the phone, or speaking from another room.

**SFX:**      The abbreviation for sound effects. Separated from direction it is isolated at the margin, abbreviated, capitalized and underlined.

**SPFX:**      The abbreviation for special effects such as a breakaway chair. Separated from direction it is isolated at the margin, capitalized, abbreviated and underlined.

**SOUND CUE**      General sound cues may appropriately appear in stage direction. Underlining is used to spotlight these. General sound cues might be background music or party chatter heard throughout a given scene.

**CAMERA CUE**      Specific instructions for the camera such as HOLD, CLOSE ON, etc. Used in direction, they are spotlighted by underlining.

**(V.O.)**
**VOICE OVER**      The mechanical transmission of a voice such as over a telephone, or on a P.A. system. The camera is usually not on the person speaking but might be if the character is thinking out loud. Stated VOICE OVER in direction and (V.O.) next to the character cue.

**(O.C.)**      A character speaking from another room or adjacent area while the camera is on some one or some thing else. The OFF CAMERA character is readily available to be on camera. Abbreviated O.C. in direction and (O.C.) next to the character cue. Note: (O.S.) or off screen is used in film formats.

Preliminaries

While margin and tab numbers are referenced to typewriters, word processors must be considered in this process. Programs for tape formats are not developed at this time. Therefore, it will be helpful to use line lengths and margin measurements to insure that the tape format printed out from a word processor will be correctly formatted.

Just as important as tab settings and spacing is making certain that ten pitch type (10 characters per inch) is used. Often, ten pitch does translate into computer printer spacing. Measure a section of a line. If there are ten characters (count spaces too) per inch, line lengths will be correct. Measuring margins and line lengths will also be helpful.

Remember also that line lengths will only be accurate if the line ends or cuts off where the cutoffs are indicated for dialogue and direction.


## Tape-Live (Standard) Format

Line Lengths and Margin Measurements

The line length is the total number of letters and spaces in the line. This assumes ten characters per inch. Ruler measurements are approximate in some cases but are no more than 2/16 of an inch off.

        Direction - 31 characters
        Dialogue - 31 characters

Measurements:

        Direction - 3 inches
        Dialogue - 3 inches

From the left edge of the paper:

        Set Heading - 1 inch
        Direction - 1 inch
        Personal Direction - 1 inch
        Dialogue - 1 1/2 inch

From the top down and the bottom up:

        Page # - 3/4 inch down from top edge of paper
        Average page length - 1 inch up from bottom of paper

## Three-Camera (Variation Format)

Line Length and Margin Measurements

             Direction - 66 characters
             Dialogue - 40 characters

Measurements:

             Direction - 6 1/2 inches long
             Dialogue - 4 inches long

From the left edge of the paper:

             Set Heading - 1 inch in
             Direction - 1 inch in
             Dialogue - 2 1/4 inches in
             Character Cue - 3 1/2 inches in

From the top down and the bottom up:

             Page # - 3/4 inch down from top edge of paper
             Average page length - 1 inch up from bottom of paper

TYPEWRITER SETTINGS:  TAPE-LIVE FORMAT

Preliminaries

Tape-Live Format distinguishes itself by the considerable space on the right side of the page which allows for notes by the director and other production personnel.  It is essentially a left sided format.  Occasionally the script is typed in the same format but is positioned on the right-hand side of the page with space on the left-hand side for director's notes.  This format shift serves to aid left-handed directors.

Set headings are capitalized, underlined and isolated at the left margin.  Stage direction and personal direction are capitalized, enclosed in parentheses, single spaced at the direction margin. Dialogue, indented slightly from the direction margin, is upper/lower case and double spaced for ease of reading.

Format

Tabs  (11, 16, 31, 73)

Breakdown                                                    Cutoffs

11 - Set heading, stage direction                            41

16 - Dialogue                                                46

31 - Character cue

73 - Page number

## COVER DESIGN:  ALL TAPED FORMATS

There are no hard fast rules governing the weight of the covers on a taped television show.  Some sitcoms utilize a simple paper cover, others use the heavier standard card stock cover generally used on scripts.  Spec scripts should be bound with the hard cover since it provides a more finished, professional look.

The amount and type of information found on a cover will vary according to type of show.  Series shows, because many different episodes are handled during the filming season, will need specific pieces of information such as series title, episode title, writer and possibly the production number, production company with address, director, draft and date.

### Series Title:
If the script is a taped, series television show the name of the series will appear on line 25 -- approximately a third of the way down from the top of the page -- centered from left to right. (This title may have to be moved up considerably if several lines of information are required on the cover)  The series title will probably be "printed" in a quick type setup on a copy machine.

### Episode Title and Author:
Triple spaced down from the SERIES TITLE and centered, the episode title is stated in upper/lower case surrounded by quotes.  "Written by" is triple spaced down and centered below that with the name of the author double spaced down, still centered.  If there are two authors they should be listed on separate lines using the word "and" to separate them.

### Production Number and/or Story Number:
Still in centered format the production number or story number. Double spacing used.

### Production Company Name:
If only the name of the production company is used (and not the address), it is placed in the lower left hand corner on line 56 or 58 at margin (11)... approximately 1 1/2 inches in from the left edge of the paper.

If the address is used as well, this block of information will need to be raised beginning on 54 or so to accommodate the additional information.

### Draft:
The draft designation is always used and is slugged in the lower right hand corner across from the production company name.  The draft -- FIRST DRAFT, FINAL DRAFT, REVISED FINAL DRAFT, etc., is always capitalized and underlined at approximately tab (56).

### Date:
The current date falls single spaced beneath the draft in upper/ lower case with the month spelled out.

### Special Note on Format:
The above placements do frequently depend on the amount and length of the information required.  There will be times when one's own best judgment must be used.

# HIGH N' DRY

"The Complaint Department"

Written by

Rich Reinhart

#07316-0

Larkin Productions
1438 N. Gower Street
Los Angeles, CA 90028

FIRST DRAFT
March 16, 1981

SAM AND SALLY

"Sam Meets Sally Mann"

#60233-066

Written by

William Gibson

Buddy Doyle

Produced by

Robert Johnson

Dan Smith

Supervising Producers

William Gibson

Buddy Doyle

Executive Producers

Greg Thompson

Gordon Thompson

WORLDWIDE PICTURES CORPORATION
5451 Marathon Street
Hollywood, CA 90038

SHOOTING SCRIPT
29 January 1981

## LAYING OUT THE FLY PAGE

The fly page (or title page) layout is the same for both Tape-Live and Three-Camera formats.

## Preliminaries

With most of the necessary production information appearing on the cover of the script where it is quickly and easily seen, there is frequently little need to use a fly page. However, the fly page does serve the purpose of displaying additional information that would not be seen on the cover. Most production companies wish to use a disclaimer outlining certain restrictions against using or duplicating the material. There is no universal format for a disclaimer but normally it would be single spaced (upper/lower case usually) beneath the centered information. Certainly, there will be duplication of information from the cover since the series title, episode title, writer, other production personnel, production company, draft and date will necessarily appear.

OAK STREET, U.S.A.

"Life's Reward"

Written by

Stephen Brice

Directed by

Ramone Preston

Saluki Productions
1894 Sepulveda
Hollywood, CA 90028

FINAL DRAFT
March 11, 1982

Preliminary Note

The material that would normally appear after the fly or title
page, if one is used, falls in the category of special pages
sometimes referred to as "front pages".

Most taped scripts will contain some or all of the following:
Staff and Crew lists, Cast Page, Sets Page, Taping and Rehearsal
Schedules, Short Rundown and Long Rundown.  (The Long Rundown is
stapled separately and is not placed in the script.)

Some or all of these various pages are needed in scripts for
shows currently in production.  Sitcoms will normally use a Cast
Page and Short Rundown whereas specials and award shows will
require all the "front pages."

These special pages will be discussed in detail later in this
Guide.  For now, we will move into the body of the script.

ACT BEGINNINGS - TAPE-LIVE FORMAT

Preliminaries

Shows written for television are divided into acts. A half-hour
sitcom will consist of a "tease" or prologue (less than two pages),
two acts and a tag (less than two pages).

Format - First Page

The beginning of an act must always FADE IN: It is slugged at
margin (11), capitalized, underlined and punctuated with a colon.
The FADE IN: for ACT ONE may not always appear on the same line from
script to script since the FADE IN: line depends on how much page
heading information is necessary above it. Usually it falls on line
12 or 14. Just remember that FADE IN: should be spaced 4 lines down
from the last line of heading information. (See example
opposite.) In other acts it will be placed 4 lines down from the
centered words ACT TWO, ACT THREE, etc.

All pages in taped television shows must be numbered including the
first page of the script. (The first page of a screenplay is not
numbered.) The first page distinguishes itself in that the series
title, the episode title, the act disposition and often the scene
number will appear here.

Note: As with all scripts broken into acts, there must be a FADE
IN: at the beginning of an act and a FADE OUT. at the end of that
act. When an act fades in, it must fade out at the end.

Tabs and Spacing - Series with Scenes

    1)  Page number - line 4, tab (73).

    2)  "SERIES TITLE" - line 6, centered, capitalized in quotes.

    3)  "Episode Title" - line 8, centered in upper/lower case and
        in quotes.

    4)  ACT ONE - line 10, centered, capitalized, and underlined.

    5)  Scene 1 - line 12, centered, upper/lower, and underlined.

    6)  FADE IN: line 12, centered, upper/lower, and underlined.

    7)  FIRST SCENE/SET HEADING - line 18, capitalized, and
        underlined.

    (See Example opposite)

Tabs and Spacing - Series without Scene Numbering

    1)  Page number - same as above, line 4.

    2)  "Episode Title" - line 6, centered, upper/lower case, in
        quotes.

    3)  ACT ONE - line 8, same as above.

    4)  FADE IN: line 12, same as above.

    5)  FIRST SET HEADING - line 14.

Act Two and Subsequent Acts

    The only heading required are the ACT and Scene designation.
    FADE IN: is of course required at the beginning of all acts.

Note: Scenes in sitcom scripts are numbered. However, writers of
spec scripts should not number scenes since the focus of the reader
should be on the idea and content.

<u>RUTH'S</u> (line 6)

"Dinner at Ruth's" (line 8)

<u>ACT ONE</u> (line 10)

<u>Scene 1</u> (line 12)

<u>FADE IN</u>:  (line 16)

<u>INT. KITCHEN - MORNING</u> (line 18)

------------------------------------------------------------

<u>ACT TWO</u> (line 6)

<u>Scene 6</u> (line 8)

<u>FADE IN</u>:  (line 12)

SET HEADINGS

Preliminaries

Set headings tell simply where and when a given sequence of action takes place.  For example:

INT. LIVING ROOM - EVENING

Set headings in taped shows serve a similar purpose as scene headings in filmed shows.  The set heading, however, is much simpler and contains less information.  In television shows, the sets are a given and the characters are stereotyped.  These two factors, the sets and the characters, are a constant.  Only the circumstances (the situation) changes.  In "Benson", for instance, the action usually takes place in either the kitchen or the governor's office and Benson is constantly trying to cover up for the governor or locking horns with Krause.

Scenes are packages of action taking place on a designated set.  Two or more consecutive scenes may take place on the same set.  Each new scene requires another set heading.  Scenes are usually designated by stating:  Scene 1, Scene 2, and so on.

Format:

   A)  All entries in the set headings are capitalized

   B)  INT. and EXT.* are abbreviated using periods

   C)  A dash with a space on either side is used to separate the elements of the heading (usually the place from the time of day)

   D)  All set headings must be underlined


REMEMBER:  When a new set is designated, that set should begin a new page.  New set, new page.




*EXT. (exterior) scenes are seldom used in taped shows since they take place in studios in interior situations.  When an exterior scene is required it usually is a set in the studio designed to look like an outdoor area.  Exterior shots may be used to establish a location where the following interior action takes place.

INT. MARIAN'S APARTMENT - DAY


JULIA'S KITCHEN - MORNING


INT. JACK'S GARAGE - LATER THAT DAY



INT. MAYOR'S OFFICE - A SHORT TIME LATER


BRENT'S LIVING ROOM - IMMEDIATELY FOLLOWING


EXT. JESSICA'S DRIVEWAY - MIDNIGHT

SET HEADINGS

Handling scenes (sets)

No use of CONTINUED

Sets or scenes flow easily from one page to the next. There is never any need to use (CONTINUED) or CONTINUED: (as in filmed shows) even though the action may cover several pages.

Rule: New set or scene = new page

When the scene is finished, a new set heading is placed on a new page. In this way the set always appears at the top of the page where it is easily seen.

CONTINUOUS ACTION

Sometimes a scene will take place in two separate areas of the same set but the action itself will be continuous. We may open the scene in a hospital room and alternate back and forth between the room and the corridor outside the room. In this case, the set is built in such a way that minimal movement of the cameras will capture the action in either the room or the corridor since essentially it is the same basic set. It is necessary though, to indicate when the action moves from one area to the next. (See Example 25A, opposite)

CONTINUOUS ACTION is also used to indicate that although we began with a conversation between two characters in the kitchen, we may cut to another scene somewhere else and later come back to the original conversation in the kitchen. This kind of situation may be referred to as IMMEDIATE PICK UP. It simply means that we continue the conversation where it left off.

LIMBO SET

Sometimes it isn't necessary to use a whole set. If a character is making a call from a pay phone, the action will take place at a "LIMBO PHONE" tucked away in a small corner of the large set. This would be slugged as a regular set heading indicating LIMBO BED, LIMBO PHONE, etc. (See Example 25B, opposite)

Note: CUT TO: will be discussed later in this Guide.

INT. HOSPITAL ROOM/CORRIDOR - NIGHT - CONTINUOUS ACTION

(LYDIA STRAINS TO HEAR THE HUSHED
CONVERSATION BETWEEN THE DOCTOR AND
NURSE IN THE CORRIDOR.  WE CUT
TO:  THE CORRIDOR)

                    DR. MIRA

What about Wednesday night?

                    NURSE

Do you think that's the right

time?

(CUT TO:  HOSPITAL ROOM WHERE LYDIA
IS CRAWLING ACROSS THE FLOOR TO THE
DOOR TO HEAR CONVERSATION BETTER)

25B – Limbo Set

LIMBO PHONE - WARREN'S OFFICE

(WARREN QUICKLY DIALS)

<u>CUT TO: AND DISSOLVE TO:  (SCENE ENDINGS)</u>


Preliminaries

When the action in a particular scene/set is finished, an ending is
used.  CUT TO:  is possibly the most often used ending to indicate
that new action in a new set will be taking place.  DISSOLVE TO:  is
another appropriate and frequently used ending.



Format

All scene/set endings appear capitalized, underlined, and punctuated
with a colon.  For the most part scene/set endings do not appear in
parentheses as does the stage direction.  In this way, the ending is
set apart from the direction.  Some production personnel do prefer
that endings be placed in parentheses and of course capitalized,
punctuated with a colon but not underlined.  (See Example 27A,
opposite)



A Note About FREEZE FRAME.

Occasionally FREEZE FRAME. might be used in a taped show, probably
at the end of an act or at the end of the show.  This term may be
thought of and even used as a scene ending.  However, FREEZE FRAME.
actually works as a camera cue which will probably be followed by
FADE OUT.  FREEZE FRAME. then should  appear isolated at the left
margin,  double spaced down,  capitalized and punctuated with a
period.  (See Example 27B, opposite)

7A - Scene Endings

(... AND ON CHARLIE'S PUZZLED LOOK
WE:)

CUT TO:

OR

         HELEN

I had completely forgotten what

a total idiot he is.

         JOHN

Selective amnesia.

(CUT TO:)

OR

(AS SHE NERVOUSLY BACKS OUT OF THE
DOOR WE:)

DISSOLVE TO:

27B - FREEZE FRAME.

(ON HER EVIL SMILE WE:)

FREEZE FRAME.

FADE OUT.

END OF ACT TWO

## ACT ENDINGS:  FADE IN: AND FADE OUT.

### Preliminaries

While scenes and sets within an act end as discussed previously with
CUT TO:  or DISSOLVE TO:, the act itself must also end and that
ending is always FADE OUT.  (Remember that the act begins with a
FADE IN: so there must be a FADE OUT.)  After FADE OUT. has been
stated to end the act, it is also necessary to indicate that this is
the END OF ACT ONE or END OF ACT TWO and so on.

### Format

FADE OUT. like its counterpart, FADE IN: is capitalized, underlined
and punctuated by a period at margin (11).  The most important and
hopefully obvious difference is the punctuation.  FADE IN: requires
a colon, indicating something to come.  FADE OUT., on the other
hand, takes a period denoting that "this is all there is of this
part."  (See Example 29A, opposite)

After the FADE OUT., it is necessary to indicate the particular act
that ·is ending.  Stated 4 lines down from FADE OUT., centered,
capitalized and underlined, should appear the words:  END OF ACT ONE
or END OF ACT TWO and so on.  (See Example 29A, opposite)

Note:  A similar notation is made at the end of the show, which
would be the TAG page in a sitcom by simply stating:  THE END
capitalized, underlined, and centered 4 lines down from FADE OUT.
(See Example 29B, opposite)

29A - END OF ACT

(FRED IS CONVINCED THAT THE SCHEME
WILL WORK AND HE ROCKS HAPPILY IN
HIS ROCKING CHAIR)

FADE OUT.

END OF ACT ONE

--------------------------------------------------------------------

29B - END OF SCRIPT

FADE OUT.

THE END

## STAGE DIRECTION

### Preliminaries

Stage direction in taped format serves the same basic purpose as stage direction in filmed format. Taped format consists of short scene and character descriptions along with camera cues, occasionally sound cues, and whatever other information might be necessary to set the mood or further describe the fabric of the scene or set. Usually direction is quite short in taped series shows since the characters are well-defined and the dialogue carries that character's personality.

Stage direction in taped format is usually only a few lines long -- much shorter and less detailed than stage direction in filmed format for good reasons. The taping situation is limited by the circumstances of the sound stage. For example, characters and sets in a taped series are well-established requiring little need for elaborate description. Dialogue plays a more significant part in carrying the story line in this situation. In filmed shows, many different locations are frequently used requiring longer and more detailed stage direction to set the scene.

In taped format, brief camera cues, occasionally sound cues, and other information necessary to set the mood are included in stage direction, i.e., whatever needs to be said to get things going for the scene.


### Format

Rule:   All stage direction in taped format is capitalized, single spaced, and in parentheses.

It is double spaced below the set heading and extends only five spaces past the middle of the page.

Tab (11)   Cutoff (41)

Notice that the end parenthesis eliminates the need for a period. Other punctuation such as a question mark, colon, or ellipsis (three periods) should appear inside the paren. (See examples opposite)

-31-

INT. MARY'S APARTMENT - DAY

(MARY IS FUSSING WITH A PLANT
WHICH IS MORE DEAD THAN ALIVE.
GEORGE IS SITTING AT THE DESK
INVOLVED WITH A STACK OF
PAPERWORK.  HE IS NOT HAPPY
ABOUT SOMETHING)

INT. CLASSROOM - LATE AFTERNOON

(ONE LONELY STUDENT IS HUNCHED
OVER HIS DESK LABORIOUSLY
WORKING.  HE DOES NOT LOOK UP AS
THE DOOR QUIETLY OPENS AND JOKO
STEPS INSIDE AND MOVES QUICKLY
OVER TO THE DESK.  WILL THIS BE
THE CONFRONTATION?)

## STAGE DIRECTION:  UNDERLINING

### Know What To Underline

Underlining is the means used in direction to spotlight specific technical instructions such as camera cues and indications of continuous sounds.  Major sound effects are discussed later on page 34.

### Underline Camera Cues

Specific camera instructions or camera cues are not often used in taped television shows such as sitcoms or soap operas, but when they do appear, they must be spotlighted by underlining.  Words such as FOLLOW or REVEAL, or STAY WITH, or HOLD are considered camera cues, along with the more obvious ones such as MOVE IN CLOSE or PULL BACK TO FIND.  (See Example 33A, opposite)

Note:  Sometimes a character's name is underlined when he first appears.  (See Example 33B, opposite)

### Underline Generalized Sound Cues

Before discussing sound cues as such, it is necessary to distinguish between generalized sound cues and sound cues that fall into the category of sound effects.  Generalized sound cues are those sounds that are, for the most part, continuous and tend to serve as background.  The most common of these would be music playing or rain falling.  These are the kinds of sound cues that might be found in direction and therefore require underlining.  (See Example 33C, opposite)

### Note:  AD LIB

Remember that AD LIB must be underlined in direction.  This term functions somewhat like a sound direction or generalized sound cue even though it is achieved by actors and actresses on the set as the tape is rolling.  (See Example 33D, opposite)

### 33A - Camera Cues

(WALKING TO THE WINDOW WENDEL
KNOWS HE'S BEEN HAD.  <u>MOVE IN
CLOSE</u> TO REVEAL HIS LOOK OF
UTTER RESIGNATION)


(FRANKIE HAS FINALLY MADE HIS
DECISION.  <u>PAN HIM TO THE DOOR</u>
AS HE LEAVES THE PARTY)


### 33B - Character Entrance

(<u>LAURA</u> ENTERS DRESSED FOR HER
DATE)


### 33C - Generalized Sound Cues

(THE <u>MUSIC CONTINUES</u> AS THE
DISCUSSION BECOMES MORE HEATED)


(THE <u>SOUND OF GENTLE RAIN</u> IS
HEARD THROUGHOUT THE REST OF THE
SCENE)


### 33D - AD LIB

(THE GUESTS <u>AD LIB</u> THEIR HORROR
AT THE SPAGHETTI OOZING DOWN THE
FRONT OF ALLISON'S EXPENSIVE
GOWN)

## STAGE DIRECTION:   UNDERLINE AND ISOLATE

Underline Specific Sound Effects, Isolate at Margin

Specific sound effects requiring technical reproduction of some kind
are handled differently than generalized sound cues.  Each sound
effect must be isolated at the margin (11), double spaced down from
the previous line, underlined, and stated, using the abbreviation
SFX:.   Double spacing must also be used after stating the sound
effect.  (See Example 35A, opposite)

If the sound effect continues onto a second line, single space down
and indent to the first letter of the first word of the effect.
(See Example 35A, opposite)


Underline Special Effects, Isolate at Margin

Any special effects required in a scene are those illusions that
require a form of prop alteration to produce a sight "gag" or a
visual facsimile.  A breakaway chair is an example.

Special effects are handled in the same format as specific sound
effects.  When stating special effects, however, the abbreviation
SPFX: is used.  Again, the SPFX: is isolated at the margin, double
spaced down from the previous line, and underlined.  Double spacing
down is also used after stating the special effect.  (See Example
35B, opposite)


Spotting Errors

If a special effect does happen to appear in the body of the
direction itself, it must be isolated at the margin in the format
outlined above.

---

| 35A - Specific Sound Effects |
|---|

(AS SHE FINISHES HER DRINK SHE
IS STARTLED BY:)

SFX:   BREAKING GLASS


(THE SILENCE IS DISTURBED BY:)

SFX:   EXCRUCIATINGLY NOISY SIREN
KLAXON-HORN TYPE


| 35B - Special Effects |
|---|

(THE FRONT DOOR CLOSES AS KEVIN
AND DIANE LEAVE FOR THE PARTY.
CAMERA PANS TO BEDROOM DOOR AND
WE SEE:)

SPFX:   SMOKE DRIFTS IN FROM
UNDER DOOR


(GEORGIE LOOKS ON IN UTTER
ASTONISHMENT AS:)

SPFX:   THE PLANT GROWS TO CEILING

## STAGE DIRECTION:  ABBREVIATIONS

General Comments

General abbreviations are perfectly acceptable in stage direction...
personal titles for example.  There are, however, a few specific
terms that require abbreviations.  These three are:

Rule:  Always abbreviate:

      1)    F.G.   (FOREGROUND)

      2)    B.G.   (BACKGROUND)

      3)    O.C.   (OFF CAMERA)*

Notice that:

      A)   These abbreviations are capitalized using periods
           after each letter.  It is appropriate that they be
           capitalized since they appear in direction which is
           capitalized.

      B)*  OFF CAMERA (O.C.) is the correct term used in tele-
           vision taped script formats.  O.S. (OFF SCREEN) is the
           term used in screenplays or filmed shows.

(See Examples opposite)

(JACK SHOOTS MARBLES ON THE FLOOR
IN THE F.G. AS MARY PACES)


(THE DOOR IN THE B.G. OPENS AND
JULIETTE POKES HER HEAD IN)


(MACK SHOUTS TO JOE O.C.)


(WE HEAR A SCUFFLING SOUND O.C.
THROUGHOUT THIS SCENE)

## STAGE DIRECTION:  MISCELLANEOUS NOTES

When Paragraphing Occurs

Paragraphing in direction in a taped show is rare since the brevity of the direction seldom warrants it.  If paragraphing should occur, however, each paragraph is isolated by itself in parentheses with double spacing used between paragraphs.  (See Example 39A, opposite)

Ellipsis (...) and Dashes ( -- )

Ellipsis and dashes are devices used to signal a change in thought or to indicate words or thoughts that are "understood" and therefore not stated.  When using the ellipsis, leave a space after the third period... When using the two dashes -- leave a space on either side.  (See Example 39B, opposite)

Rule for Breaking Direction From One Page to the Next

Direction may be broken from one page to the next as long as the break occurs at the end of a sentence.

Rule:  **Never** break a sentence from one page to the next.

The same principle applies as in paragraphing.  Close the parenthesis at the end of the sentence... Remember that a period is not required at the end of that sentence.  On the next page, the next sentence of the direction begins by restating the parenthesis.  In effect, it works the same way as two paragraphs.

Spotting Errors:  No form of scene CONTINUED is necessary.  (See Example 39C, opposite)

## 39A - Paragraphing

(MARION IS AT HER WRITING DESK
INDULGING IN MORE DAYDREAMING
THAN WRITING.  SHE FINALLY GIVES
UP ON THE WRITING, GETS UP AND
MOVES AIMLESSLY OVER TO GAZE OUT
THE WINDOW)

(A FEW MOMENTS LATER, WILLIAM
ENTERS FROM THE HALLWAY WITH A
TOWEL WRAPPED AROUND HIM)

## 39B - Ellipses and Dashes

(TOMMY SITS ON THE BENCH LOOKING
VERY LONELY AND ABANDONED... IS
LIFE REALLY SUPPOSED TO BE THIS
DIFFICULT?)

(RUTH FINALLY CATCHES ON TO THE
IMPLICATION OF DAVE'S WORDS --
SHE'S NO DUMMY)

## 39C - Breaking Direction

(KATHY HOLDS THE BRIEFCASE
TIGHTLY TRYING TO THINK OF THE
PERFECT PLACE TO STASH IT.  SHE
LOOKS AROUND THE KITCHEN HOPING
FOR DIVINE INSPIRATION.  THE
REFRIGERATOR.  PULLING OPEN THE
DOOR, SHE BEGINS REARRANGING THE
FOOD ITEMS TO CREATE SPACE FOR
THE BRIEFCASE)

------------------------- next page ----------------------------

7.

(THE BACK DOOR OPENS AND MARGE
WALKS IN CARRYING A FRESHLY
BAKED CAKE)

STAGE DIRECTION:  TITLES OF SONGS AND BOOKS

General Comments

Whenever a song or book title is used in direction, it should be set in quotation marks.  This serves to set the title apart so that it does not get lost in the direction.  Occasionally, the title is underlined as well, but for most practical purposes it is not necessary to use such heavy-handed means to point out a song or book.  (See Example 41A and 41B, opposite)

Quotation marks are also used to enclose a message or words that are to appear on a sign or banner.  In this particular case it may be legitimate to underline that information as well since it serves as a cue to the property department which will be responsible for creating the sign.  An example of this might be the necessity of a banner stating "WELCOME HOME, LIZ".  (See Example 41C, opposite)


Note  These same procedures are used in dialogue but retaining the upper/lower case format and capitalizing the first letter of each major, important word in the book or song title.

## 41A - Titles of Songs

(MARC DRIFTS INTO THE KITCHEN
HOLDING A BOUQUET OF DAFFODILS,
WHISTLING, "ISN'T IT ROMANTIC")

## 41B - Titles of Books

(ROCKO PUMPS THE PATIENT UP
HIGHER IN THE DENTIST CHAIR.  HE
THEN TURNS AROUND TO THE COUNTER
BEHIND HIM AND PICKS UP A
BOOK.  AS HE SLOWLY TURNS BACK
TO THE PATIENT WE SEE THAT HE IS
READING "BEGINNING DENTISTRY")

## 41C - Signs and Banners

(MAUDE AND CORA HOLD UP A SIGN THAT
SAYS, "CONGRATULATIONS, HENRY")

The stage direction composite
on the following page illustrates
the elements previously discussed.

INT. LIVING ROOM - NIGHT

(A FEW MOMENTS THEN WE HEAR AN
O.C. HUMMING AS FRED COMES
NONCHALANTLY DOWN THE STAIRS.
HE CONTINUES HUMMING AS HE
SEARCHES FOR THE HIDDEN MONEY)

SFX:  KEY BEING INSERTED IN FRONT
      DOOR AND LOCK BEING TURNED

(THERE'S NO TIME TO HIDE.  DONNA
STEPS INSIDE AND STARES, ARMS
CROSSED, AS FRED AD LIBS
GREETINGS)

(DONNA IS SUSPICIOUS.  FRED
BEGINS TO DANCE WHILE WHISTLING,
"TEA FOR TWO".  AFTER A MOMENT
IT IS OBVIOUS THAT THIS PLOY
WON'T WORK.  SHE REACHES FOR A
BOOK TO THROW AT HIM.  IT IS
TITLED, "THE COMPLETE MAN".  AS
SHE AIMS AND THROWS IT:)

SPFX:  BOOK OPENS AND BOTTLE OF
       BOOZE FALLS OUT

(SHE KICKS THE BOTTLE ASIDE,
TURNS AND WALKS OUT AS:)

# CHARACTER CUES

## Preliminaries

The character cue is simply the name of the character to whom lines of dialogue are assigned.  Either the first name or the last name may be used.  It may even be appropriate to use the whole name.  A given character may not be named but may be referred to by his title or by a specific role, only, however, if that is a minor role.

## Format

The character cue is always stated in capital letters at tab (32).  (See Example 45A, opposite)

## Abbreviate Personal Titles.

Personal titles are abbreviated in the character cue.  It helps keep the character cue short.  (See Example 45B, opposite)

## Use of (V.O.) and (O.C.)

(V.O.) or VOICE OVER means that the character is not usually seen on screen but we hear his voice conveyed over some kind of mechanical contrivance such as a telephone or tape recorder.  The situation may be one where the character is thinking out loud.  We will hear that character's voice on a pre-recorded sound tape while the camera is on the character.  When a character speaks on the telephone as a (V.O.) we would not see that character but would merely hear the voice.

(O.C.) or OFF CAMERA means that the character is not seen on the screen but we hear him talking from another room in a house or from some adjacent area.  In an (O.C.) situation the character is readily available to be on camera.  Both (V.O.) and (O.C.) appear capitalized in parentheses, abbreviated with periods beside the character cue.  (See Example 45C, opposite)

45A - Character Cue as a Specific Role

>MELANY

>WAITER

>LADY IN RED

>MUGGER

45B - Character Cue With Personal Title

>COL. HOLLINGSWORTH

>DR. SPOCK

>FATHER MURPHY

45C - Use of (V.O.) and (O.S.)

>RAY (V.O.)

(OVER PHONE)

This is a bad connection.  I

can hardly hear you.


(COL. POTTS WALKS AWAY FROM GROUP)

>COL. POTTS (O.C.)

Look over here.


OR

(CAMERA MOVES IN CLOSE ON MARY AS
JOHN SAYS:)

>JOHN (O.C.)

What are you thinking?

## CHARACTER CUE

Specific Roles Are Placed In Parentheses

The specific role of a character may be designated in the character
cue along with the character name.  This is particularly useful in
variety shows where various skits are used.  The role information
should appear capitalized in parentheses beside the character cue.
(See Example 47A, opposite)


Numbers to Indicate Minor Characters Playing Same Role

If there is more than one character playing the same role, it should
be designated by using the number sign and numbered thusly, #1, #2,
#3 and so on.  This information appears beside the character cue.
(See Example 47B, opposite)

| 47A - Character Cue With Role Designation |
| --- |

WILLIAM (CLOWN)

MYCROFT (DETECTIVE)

| 47B - Several Characters in the Same Role |
| --- |

POLICEMAN #2

WARRIOR #5

INMATE #3

PERSONAL DIRECTION

Preliminaries

Personal direction consists of those special, usually short, instructions intended for a specific character and apply only to that character. In three-camera formats, the main function of personal direction serves to cue the character on stage (ENTERS) or sends him away (EXITS) and in general guides his physical actions to fit in with the goings on of the scene: (LOOKS AT HIS WATCH) (READS OVER HER SHOULDER) (STEPS BACK). There will of course be some references to guide the mood of the character to fit the action: (FEELS TOTALLY HELPLESS) (SMUGLY OPENS THE BOX) (LAUGHS).

Format

Personal direction is handled in exactly the same way as stage direction. Always capitalized in parentheses, personal direction appears at the margin (11) and is single spaced. All the rules that apply to stage direction apply here. (See Example 49A, opposite)

Use of (CONT'D) When Another Character's Personal Direction Interrupts Dialogue

The personal direction for another character may be interjected in the original character's dialogue. That other character's personal direction must be stated at the margin in the correct format as above, but the character cue of the original character must be restated with (CONT'D) beside the name. (See Example 49B, opposite)

49B - Format

                    PAULINE

          Are you telling me that I have

          to sacrifice my parking space

          for this so-called promotion?

(STARTS TOWARDS DOOR)

          I'd rather have the parking

          space.


49B - Use of CONT'D When Personal Direction Interrupts Dialogue

                    JENNIFER

(PUNCHING TIME CARD)

          Good morning, Mr. Robbins.

                    ROBBINS

(SARCASTIC)

          Glad to see you could finally

          make it in this morning.

(SHE STOPS, LOOKS UP)

                    ROBBINS (CONT'D)

          You look awfully nice... but

          then I suppose you had all that

          extra time...

                    JENNIFER

(UNCOVERING TYPEWRITER)

          You can't expect me to look

          like this and be on time both.

PERSONAL DIRECTION

<u>Rule</u>:  Don't End a Page With Personal Direction

When breaking dialogue (discussed on page 54) from one page to the
next, the break should be made before personal direction.  In this
way, the personal direction will fall more appropriately at the top
of the next page before the continuation of the speech.  (See
Example 51A, opposite)

51A - Don't End a Page With Personal Direction

                    MURRAY

          I've got it!  I've got the

          evidence right here.

                    (MORE)


-------------------------- next page ---------------------------

                                                          6.


                    MURRAY (CONT'D)
          (HOLDS UP RATTY SHEATH OF PAPERS)
          Ace, take these over to the

          D.A.'s office and tell him

          we've got a bird in the hand.

## DIALOGUE

### Preliminaries

Dialogue consists of all those words and utterances said by the character. Dialogue may be the most important element of a script since characters' interactions with one another and reactions to people, situations, and events are the vehicle by which a production moves. Therefore, dialogue should not be "tampered with" by anyone but the writer or other production personnel.

### Format

The format rules governing dialogue are devised to make the dialogue clear and easy to read. Visually, the lines of dialogue appear slightly off center to the left of the page. Double spacing is used along with upper/lower case type. Dialogue begins at tab (16) and cuts off at (51). The cutoff will sometimes run a few letters under or over since hyphenation of words in dialogue is NOT ALLOWED. (See Example 53A, opposite)

53A - Dialogue Placement

INT. KITCHEN - MORNING

(THE GOVERNOR IS SEATED AT THE
TABLE, FINISHING BREAKFAST.  MARIA
POURS ANOTHER CUP OF COFFEE FOR HIM
AND THEN STARTS TO CLEAR DISHES)

                    GOVERNOR

    Oh, Miss Cortez, that French toast

    was delicious.

(HANSON ENTERS)

                    MARIA

    That wasn't French toast, that was

    Toast a la Maria.

                    GOVERNOR

    What's the difference?

                    HANSON

    You dip it in the batter and then

    you aggravate it for about twenty

    minutes.

(MARIA GIVES HIM A LOOK)

## DIALOGUE RULES

Follow Precise Spelling and Grammatical Rules

Most of the following rules can also be found in Appendix B, page 157, called "Universal Truths". Many of these rules are those of standard grammar, others concern those special considerations peculiar to dialogue.

(a) Spell out:

   1) One and two digit numbers. (Three or more digit numbers may be written numerically, also license numbers and telephone numbers.)

   2) Personal titles, except for Mr., Mrs., and Ms.

   3) Indications of time. Example: one-thirty.

   4) Okay, and all other words it might be tempting to abbreviate such as doctor. When in doubt, spell it out.

(b) No Hyphenation

   Words may not be hyphenated from one line to the next. Those words which are normally hyphenated may be extended to the next line. Example: son-in-law.

(c) Never break a sentence from one page to the next. End the sentence before moving to the next page.

(d) Pauses in a sentence may be indicated with the ellipsis (three periods). A space should be left after the third period.

(See Example 55A, opposite)

(e) The ellipsis is also used when a sentence is interrupted by personal direction. In this case, the ellipsis must appear both at the end break and at the beginning of the remainder of the sentence.

(See Example 55A, opposite)

(f) Pauses may also be indicated by using two dashes. Leave a space on each side of them.

(See Example 55B, opposite)

(g) Paragraphing is occasionally used in long passages of dialogue. The author dictates where it should occur.

## 55A - The Ellipsis as a Pause

                    ELLIE
(WORKING CROSSWORD PUZZLE)
    What's a...
(COUNTING)
    ... six, seven letter word for
    a Lithuanian monkey wrench.
                    MARGE
    Let's see... I came across that
    word yesterday... let me
    think...


## 55B - Dashes Used as a Pause

                    JONATHAN
    I know you've been under a
    great deal of stress lately --
    but sitting naked in this
    grapefruit tree -- somehow
    isn't going to solve anything.

## USE OF (MORE) AND (CONT'D)

### Breaking Dialogue: When to Use (MORE)

When a character has a lengthy dialogue which must be continued onto the next page,* the dialogue must be broken at the end of a sentence. (If it's a stream of consciousness speech with no punctuation other than pauses, the break should be made at the pause.) To indicate that additional dialogue will appear on the next page, the term (MORE) is used. (MORE) applies only to dialogue.

#### Format Rules

1) (MORE) always appears in caps and parentheses, double spaced down from the last sentence of dialogue.

2) (MORE) is logically stated on the character cue tab (31) since it is the character who is to have _more_ lines. (See Example 57A, opposite)

### How to Use (CONT'D)

After stating (MORE) at the bottom of the page to indicate more dialogue, the term (CONT'D) must be stated next to the restated character cue at the top of the next page. (See Example 57B, opposite)

#### Format Rules

1) (CONT'D) always appears capitalized and abbreviated in parentheses.

2) (CONT'D) always appears beside the character cue.

   Note: (CONT'D) is the only use of the word "continued" in taped formats, and it applies only to dialogue/character.

---

\* Frequently, television shows will request that dialogue _not_ be broken from page to page. In this case then, if the dialogue is too long to fit in the space left on the page, it must begin on the next page even though it leaves more space than usual at the bottom of the preceding page.

57A - Use of (MORE) and (CONT'D) When Breaking Dialogue

11.

               RICHARD
Look at this mess.  No
consideration.  It's bad enough
to be robbed but do they <u>always</u>
have to leave a mess.
               (MORE)


-------------------------- next page ----------------------------

12.

               RICHARD (CONT'D)
And look at that!  They didn't
take the stereo.  Why didn't
they take the stereo?  That's a
good stereo.  Just goes to show
you they had no taste on top of
it all.

## USE OF (CONT'D)

(a)      Use of (CONT'D) When Interrupted by Stage Direction

In sitcoms dialogue is often interrupted by an intervening stage direction or personal direction. (Remember that personal direction is handled the same as stage direction.) If more than four lines of stage direction interrupt the dialogue it is necessary to restate the character cue again so that there is no question to whom the lines belong. When the character cue is stated again, the term (CONT'D) must be used next to it in the same format as discussed previously. (See Example 59A, opposite)

(b)      Use of (CONT'D) When Interrupted by Another Character's Personal Direction

The character (CONT'D) must be used when another character's personal direction interrupts the dialogue. This again, serves to make clear that someone has personal direction in the midst of all this dialogue and that the dialogue of the original character is to continue. (See Example 59B, opposite)


Note: This use of (CONT'D) regarding interruption by stage and personal direction is somewhat flexible, depending upon production needs. Some shows prefer that (CONT'D) be used only after four lines of interrupting stage direction. (CONT'D) is never required after the character's own personal direction. The rule of thumb is, if no special instructions are given, use (CONT'D) wherever it will save confusion and promote clarity.

59A - When Interrupted by Stage Direction

                    MARK

What do you think?

(MARK THROWS UP HIS HANDS IN A
GESTURE OF HOPELESSNESS.  JOHN
STANDS UP AND PRESSES THE INTERCOM
BUTTON)

                    MARK (CONT'D)

Maggie, please come in here a

minute.

59B - When Interrupted by Another Character's Personal Direction

                    JOHN

You better get down there right

away.

(MARK JUMPS UP FROM HIS CHAIR AND
HEADS FOR THE DOOR)

                    JOHN (CONT'D)

I'll meet you there after I

talk to Murphy.

JOE'S GARAGE

"Joe's Brush With Culture"

ACT ONE


FADE IN:

INT. GARAGE - DAY

(JOE ENTERS THROUGH DOOR)

(APPLAUSE)

(HE CROSSES TO THE COKE MACHINE,
KICKS THE SIDE AND WE HEAR:)

SFX:  BOTTLE DESCENDING

(JOE REMOVES A BOTTLE OF BOURBON
FROM THE MACHINE.  HE UNCAPS THE
BOTTLE AND TAKES A SWIG)

                    JOE

    And to think some people

    actually drink coffee!

(JOE BEGINS TO SEARCH AROUND THE
TABLE AND WORKING AREA)

                    JOE (CONT'D)

    Now, where the heck is that

    darn newspaper?

(A VAN PULLS IN AND A UNIFORMED
DRIVER GETS OUT)

                    JOE (CONT'D)

    A customer?  Amazing.

                    DRIVER

    Hey, you!  Joe's garage?

CUT TO:

EXT. GARAGE AREA - CONTINUOUS ACTION

(JOE MAKES A SUPERFICIAL
EXAMINATION OF THE VAN THE DRIVER
BROUGHT IN.  AS HE MOVES AROUND TO
THE FRONT OF THE VAN, HE GIVES THE
CHASSIS A KICK AND:)

SPFX:  THE GRILL FALLS OFF

(HE PROCEEDS TO OPEN THE VAN DOOR)

                    JOE

(MUTTERS TO HIMSELF)

     This is a piece of junk!

(HE OPENS THE DOOR AND THE RADIO
GOES ON)

SFX:  ROCK 'N' ROLL MUSIC

(HE QUICKLY CLOSES THE DOOR)

               JOE (CONT'D)

     Well, I'll be...

FADE OUT.


                    END OF ACT ONE

# ACT TWO

FADE IN:

INT. GARAGE - NIGHT

(JOE IS SITTING ON THE COUCH.
TRIXIE ENTERS, MOVES OVER AND SITS
NEXT TO HIM.  JOE MOVES AWAY FROM
HER.  SHE SLIDES OVER CLOSE TO HIM
AGAIN)

                    JOE

(UNCOMFORTABLE, ALL BUSINESS)

        Lionel should have that drive

        shaft fixed in a couple of hours.

                    TRIXIE

        No hurry.  What do you do for fun

        around here, honey?

(JOE SQUIRMS OVER FURTHER AWAY FROM
HER BUT HE IS TRAPPED AGAINST THE
ARM.  HE BECOMES MORE AND MORE
BUSINESS-LIKE AS THE SITUATION HEATS
UP)

                    JOE

        Shouldn't be any problem with you

        being on your way in less than two

        hours... that ought to put you in

        Carlinville in time for your

        performance... Say, why don't I

        get you a Coke... Might help pass

        the time... It's a service we

        extend to our customers free of

        charge...

                    (MORE)

                    JOE (CONT'D)

     Fact is, we keep the machine

     just for our customers...

(BUT HE'S WEDGED IN AND CAN'T QUITE
GET UP.  SHE'S GOT HIM WHERE SHE
WANTS HIM)

                    TRIXIE

     Listen, how about you and me

     splitting.  We could go into

     town and have some fun.

SFX:  DOOR OPENS

(ANGLE WIDENS TO INCLUDE LIONEL,
WHO ENTERS WIPING HIS HANDS ON A
GREASY RAG.  HAPPY FOR THE
INTERRUPTION, JOE JUMPS UP AND
MOVES OVER TO LIONEL)

                    JOE

     Got her done already, Lionel?...

     That was sure fast... wasn't as

     bad as we thought, eh?

                    LIONEL

     Nope.  Worse than we thought.

     Needs a complete overhaul.

     Can't do it tonight.  Have to

     wait 'til morning.

(ON TRIXIE'S INNOCENT SMILE AND
JOE'S LOOK OF UTTER CHAGRIN, WE:)

FADE OUT.


                    END OF ACT TWO

The following section covers
Three-Camera Format.
The emphasis is on those
elements of information that
are different from
Tape-Live Format.

## TYPEWRITER SETTINGS:  THREE-CAMERA FORMAT

Preliminaries

Three-Camera Format, as discussed before, is a second format used in taped shows.  When compared to a page of Tape-Live Format, the look of Three-Camera Format is quite different.  The stage direction extends across the page.  The personal direction appears in the dialogue, capitalized, and in parentheses.  Scenes are lettered instead of numbered.  (See pages 7 and 8)

There seems to be no particular determining factor in deciding which format is to be used, Tape-Live or Three-Camera.  It depends on whichever format the production company uses.  A writer submitting a speculation script for a current series should of course use the format used for that show.

Cover and Fly Page

Both the cover and the fly page of a Three-Camera Format Script follow the same rules and considerations as discussed in the Tape-Live Taped section.

Tabs   (11, 22, 36, 61, 73)

| Breakdown | | Cutoffs |
|---|---|---|
| 11 | Set Heading, Stage Direction | 76 |
| 22 | Dialogue | 61 |
| 36 | Character Cue | |
| 61 | Act Ending, Scene Endings | |
| 73 | Page Number | |

ACT BEGINNINGS AND SCENES

Preliminaries

Re-read the information on page 20. Acts in Three-Camera Format are
handled in the same way as acts in Tape-Live Format. The scenes,
however, are not. First, letters are used to designate the
scenes. Second, the beginning page of each scene starts about half
way down the page with the scene letter appearing about one-fourth
of the way down. The heading information appears in the same manner
as Tape-Live Format.

THE FIRST PAGE - ACT ONE - SCENE A

1) Page number - line 4, tab (73)

2) SHOW TITLE - line 6, centered, capitalized, and underlined

3) "Episode Title" - line 8, centered, upper/lower case, in quotes

4) ACT ONE - line 10, centered, capitalized, and underlined

5) SCENE LETTER - line 20, centered, capitalized, and underlined

6) FADE IN: - line 30, margin (11), capitalized, underlined, and
            punctuated with a colon.

7) First set heading line 32, capitalized, underlined in the
            usual manner

8) Cast listed in parentheses in upper/lower case

   (See Example 67A, opposite)


THE SECOND PAGE - ACT ONE - SCENE (A)

Note: The scene letter appears on all subsequent pages of the scene
directly under the page number.

1) Page number - line 4, tab (73)

2) Scene letter -beginning parenthesis on line 5, tab (73) (same
            as the page number tab), capitalized with a
            closed parenthesis.

3) First entry - Direction, Character Cue, Set Heading, etc., line
            6 at the appropriate tab.

   (See Example 67B, opposite)

1.


CAMP POTAWATAMI

"The Night of the Grizzly"

ACT ONE


<u>A</u>


FADE IN:

INT. CABIN - NIGHT
(Emilie, Roger, Scott)


-------------------------- next page ----------------------------

2.
(A)

FRANKIE

Where's Larry?

## SECOND SCENE (B)

The first page of the second scene which will be scene <u>B</u>, is handled similarly to the first page of an Act except that less information is necessary.  The title of the series and the episode title are not used.  Nor is it necessary to restate the Act.

Format

1)  Page number - line 4, tab (73)

2)  Scene letter - line 20, centered, capitalized, and underlined

3)  Set heading - line 30, at margin (11), capitalized, and underlined.

Notice that on the first page of a given scene, it is not necessary to slug the scene letter under the page number since the letter is already obviously stated on the page.  (See example opposite)

<u>Note:</u>  ACT TWO and all subsequent acts are stated on line 6 (two lines down from the page number, centered, capitalized, and underlined.

B

INT. RESTAURANT - DAY
(Jeff, Gary)

THE PLACE IS BUSY.  WAITRESSES AND WAITERS WITH TRAYS OF FOOD
MOVE THROUGH THE ROOM.  JEFF ENTERS, SITS AT THE COUNTER, AND
MOTIONS TO WAITRESS.

                    JEFF

     Coffee, please.

## SCENE AND ACT ENDINGS

The types of endings used for acts and scenes in Three-Camera Format are the same ones used in Tape-Live Format. In Three-Camera Format, however, scene endings appear on the right side of the page tab (61). (See Example 71A, opposite)

### Format

As usual, scene endings are capitalized, underlined, and punctuated with a colon. The exception in punctuation is the act ending FADE OUT. which is punctuated with a period. In Three-Camera Format these scene endings appear over on the right side of the page at tab (61). If there is confusion about where to place the scene and act endings in these two formats the position becomes clear by noting whether or not there is a tab setting over towards the right side of the page. If there is a tab setting tab (61) such as there is in Three-Camera Format it becomes obvious that scene and act endings are to appear in this spot since no other element of information is ever placed here. (In Tape-Live Format you will note that there is no tab setting tab (61); therefore, scene and act endings must logically appear on the left.)

### Long Scene Endings

If a scene ending is too long to fit on tab (61) without running off the side of the page, then the ending must be backspaced from the right margin (76). This insures that the ending will fit. (See Example 71A, opposite)

### Act Endings

Act endings are treated the same in Three-Camera Format as they are in Tape-Live Format. After FADE OUT., drop down four lines and state END OF ACT ONE, END OF ACT TWO, THE END, etc. This information is centered, capitalized, and underlined. (See Examples 75B and 75C, opposite)

### A Note About FREEZE FRAME

Occasionally FREEZE FRAME. is used in a taped show at the end of an act or at the end of the script. This term may be thought of and even incorrectly used as a scene ending. However, it actually works as a camera cue which probably will be followed by FADE OUT. FREEZE FRAME. should appear isolated at the left margin, double spaced down, capitalized, and punctuated with a period. (See Example 76C, opposite)

71A - Position of Scene Endings

DISSOLVE TO:

CUT TO:

MATCH DISSOLVE TO:

-------------------------------------------------------------------

71B - Act Ending

FADE OUT.

END OF ACT ONE

-------------------------------------------------------------------

71C - FREEZE FRAME.

FRANK AND RUTH LOOK AT EACH OTHER.

FREEZE FRAME.

FADE OUT.

THE END

## STAGE DIRECTION

### Preliminaries

All the rules that apply to stage direction in Tape-Live Format apply to Three-Camera Format. Refer to pages 32 and 34 and note that continuous, generalized sound cues and camera cues are underlined. So are AD LIB and VOICE OVER. Remember that these terms are always capitalized since they appear in direction which is normally capitalized. Anything that would be underlined in Tape-Live Format is underlined in Three-Camera Format.

### Format

Stage direction begins at margin (11) and extends across the page to the right hand margin (76). (Hyphenation of words is acceptable if not overdone.) Notice that stage direction does NOT appear in parentheses as it does in Tape-Live Format. (See example opposite)

<u>B</u>

<u>INT. CABIN - NIGHT</u>
(Bert, Larry)

BERT COMES INTO THE ROOM FROM THE STOREROOM AREA CARRYING SOME
FIREWOOD.  FROM O.C. WE <u>HEAR A MOAN</u>.  <u>WIDEN</u> TO INCLUDE LARRY
HUDDLED IN A CORNER TRYING TO KEEP WARM... WITHOUT SUCCESS.
BERT CONTINUES HIS TASK IGNORING LARRY'S <u>AD LIB</u> GRUMBLINGS.

## CHARACTER CUES

Explanation

All the Tape-Live Format rules regarding character cues apply to Three-Camera Format. (Refer to pages 44 - 46) The only difference is the placement of the character cue on the page. In Three-Camera Format the character cue appears more toward the center of the page at tab (36). The placement difference between the two formats is easily seen. (See Examples 75A and 75B, opposite)

75A - Three-Camera Format

                    JOE

Here we are.   Now this is what I call

rustic.

                    LIZ

I think it's a matter of semantics.

                    JUANITA (O.C.)

Come in the kitchen where the action is.

75B - Tape-Live Format

               GEORGE

Want to hear the new song I

wrote?

               MARY

What's it called?

               GEORGE

I haven't decided yet.

## PERSONAL DIRECTION

### Preliminaries

Personal direction in Three-Camera Format is handled differently
than in Tape-Live Format. In Three-Camera Format personal direction
appears within the parameters of the dialogue. Personal direction
is distinguished from the dialogue by capitalization and
parentheses. In many respects this method of handling the personal
direction clarifies visually, each character's own personal
instruction.

### Format

Personal direction is capitalized and in parentheses (omitting
punctuation at the ending parenthesis), within the margins of the
dialogue tab (22). Cut off (61). Two spaces are required after the
end parenthesis just as though it is the period at the end of a
sentence. Because the dialogue is double spaced, double spacing is
used for the personal direction if it extends onto the next line.
(See Example 77A, opposite)

Note: Avoid ending dialogue with lengthy personal direction. In
this case the personal direction should be pulled out to the left
side of the page to work as stage direction.

### Spotting Errors

Personal direction appearing in a specific character's dialogue
belongs to that character and that character only. An interjected
personal direction of another character must be pulled out to the
left margin to become stage direction. The original character
speaking must then be restated using (CONT'D) when he resumes
talking. (See Example 77B, opposite)

77A

NANCY

(LOOKING IN DRAWER OF TABLE)  If I don't
find it, things could get very serious!
(THEN)  Maybe it's... (MOVES TO POTTED
PLANT)  ... in some logical place... Ah
hah.  (WITH GREAT SATISFACTION)  Here we
are, just like magic.

77B

DICK

I don't think you should move there.
(JANE PAUSES, LOOKS UP)  Just trying to
be helpful.

(CORRECT EXAMPLE)

DICK

I don't think you should move there.
(JANE PAUSES, LOOKS UP)

DICK (CONT'D)

Just trying to be helpful.

## DIALOGUE

Preliminaries

All the spelling and grammatical rules that apply to dialogue in
Tape-Live Format apply to Three-Camera Format. (Refer to pages 52
and 157) Dialogue placement in Three-Camera Format, however, is not
the same; the lines are longer and more centered on the page.


Format

Dialogue begins at tab (22) and cuts off at tab (61). Double
spacing and upper/lower case type are used. (See Example 79A,
opposite)


Breaking Dialogue: Use of (MORE) and (CONT'D)

These two techniques, used to indicate dialogue broken from one page
to the next, are used in exactly the same way as Tape-Live Format.
(MORE) is used in breaking dialogue from one page to the next with
(CONT'D) on the next page beside the character cue to make clear his
continuation. (Refer to page 56)

(MORE) indicates more dialogue on the next page.
(CONT'D) must then appear on the next page beside the character cue.


Interrupted Dialogue: Use of (CONT'D)

(CONT'D) is also used when direction interrupts dialogue. (Refer to
page 57)

79A

<u>C</u>

INT. MINDY'S APARTMENT - TWO DAYS LATER
(Fred, Cora, Mindy)

FRED IS IN THE LIVING ROOM WITH CORA'S LUGGAGE.

                    FRED

        Come on, everybody.  (PICKS UP BAGS)  We

        better get going or Cora's going to miss

        her shuttle to Las Vegas.

CORA ENTERS WITH MINDY FROM THE BEDROOM.

                    CORA

        Hold your water, Fredso.

The following sample is a
composite of several pages
of Three-Camera Format.
These pages incorporate
most of the information
previously discussed.

<u>LIFE IN THE BIG CITY</u>

"Take Flight"

<u>ACT ONE</u>

<u>A</u>

<u>FADE IN</u>:

<u>INT. LARRY'S APARTMENT - DAY</u>
(Larry, Mitzi, Bert)

THIS IS A NEW, LARGER APARTMENT, WHICH OBVIOUSLY HAS JUST BEEN
PAINTED AND SPRUCED UP.  WHILE IT IS FURNISHED, THE
FURNISHINGS ARE SPARSE.  <u>MITZI ENTERS</u> FROM BEDROOM.  SHE IS
TALKING TO LARRY WHO IS <u>STILL THERE</u>.

                    MITZI

          Larry, this place is perfect for you...

          masculine... dignified... You're going to

          love living here... and with the building

          just loaded with pretty girls, you're

          going to love living here... You busy

          little fella.

                    BERT

          Come on, come on... Fresh air, babbling

          brook, open fireplace.

                    (MORE)

> BERT (CONT'D)

A chance for best friends to just relax
and enjoy each other's company. (STARTS
SINGING) "Chestnuts Roasting on an Open
Fire."

> BERT/LARRY

(SINGING TOGETHER) "Jack Frost Nipping
at your Nose..."

> LARRY

(CUTS IT OFF) No, I've got to get
settled in here... Come on, help me bring
that piece of furniture up from the
basement.

LARRY EXITS WITH TEDDY BEAR.

> BERT

In the wilderness. Roommates in the
wilderness. (THEN) Hey, Lar.

> LARRY (O.C.)

What?

> BERT

You gonna take Mr. Paws with you?

FROM O.C. LARRY THROWS MR. PAWS TO BERT. BERT THROWS IT IN BOX.

> BERT (CONT'D)

Two points.

BERT EXITS.

CUT TO:

B

INT. RECREATION ROOM - DAY
(Frankie, Carol)

FRANKIE COMES FLYING THROUGH THE DOORS ON A SKATEBOARD.  CAROL
COMES RUNNING IN AFTER HIM.

                    FRANKIE

          I'm not upset!

                    CAROL

          You are upset!

SFX:  JUKEBOX IN BACKGROUND

                    FRANKIE

          I'm not upset!

                    CAROL

          You are upset!

                    FRANKIE

          No.  I _want_ you to take the job.

ON CAROL'S LOOK WE:

The next section covers "front" pages.
These pages consist of taping schedules,
staff and crew lists, short rundowns,
long rundowns, and any other special
pages required by production personnel.

Introduction

Tape-Live Format (Standard) is used for variety, award, and special shows. However, additional information is necessary since these programs are more complex, longer and involve many more performers and production personnel than weekly sitcoms. Special shows may feature dancers, singers, and skits and may incorporate pre-taped sections, remote broadcast segments and other technical considerations such as lighting, props, and special effects. Timings for segments, commercials, promos, station I.D.'s and the like are essential. In the case of award and special shows, the production personnel is brought together for the express purpose of putting the show together. This necessitates contact lists of addresses and phone numbers.

Discussed in this section is the format for music cues, lyrics, orchestra bars, props, special effects, lighting and audience cues as well as segment slugs (headings), INTO: and OUT OF: These elements of the script are fitted into or overlaid onto the basic format.

Cover and Fly (Title) Page

The cover used on variety, award, and special show scripts follow the same rules and considerations discussed in the Tape-Live Taped section. (Page 14) If all the required information appears on the cover, a fly page may not be used.

"Front Pages"

Special shows require specific kinds of information about the script itself and also about the production personnel. Some "front" pages may appear in other taped scripts whether Tape-Live or Three-Camera Format. These pages fall into two categories: Those containing information about the actual production and those containing information about production personnel.

Following here are brief descriptions of each of these unique pages. (Colored paper is used to distinguish these special pages from the rest of the script and from one another.) Only a select few of these pages will appear in taped shows such as sitcoms. Here one would normally find a cast/set page, rehearsal schedule and a short rundown. These are not nearly as detailed and complex as the comparable pages in a variety, award, or special show. Long rundowns rarely appear in the script itself. They are stapled separately and accompany the script for distribution to certain technical personnel.

# "FRONT" PAGE DESCRIPTIONS

CAST/SETS - A listing of the cast of characters and the performers playing those characters along with a list of all the sets required for the show. Separate pages may be used for the cast and the sets.

CONTACT LIST - A listing of the production personnel working on a particular show. There are several kinds of contact lists: CAST, CREW, STAFF, PERFORMERS, etc. Some or all of these pages may be used. A contact list will contain the names, addresses and phone numbers of all persons and services employed by the production. Contact lists are found in variety, award, and special shows.

SCHEDULES - These schedules may be for REHEARSAL, BLOCKING and TAPING. Frequently, rehearsal and blocking is combined into one schedule. On these pages are listed times and places where performers must rehearse and technicians must block and tape the show. The taping schedule usually incorporates a CAST CALL which appears at the end of each taping day. This tells performers what time and where they are to appear on that particular day for make-up, wardrobe, etc.

SHORT RUNDOWN (SRD) - The short rundown is a brief listing of the scenes and/or segments (variety, awards, and specials) in the script. Each item is listed along with the cast and is referenced by the page number in the script. The SRD is kind of a table of contents for the script but works more importantly as a timing sheet. SRD's include boxes (four, five, or six) so that the timing for each segment may be indicated. The SRD should always be positioned at the end of all the "front" pages just before the body of the script.

LONG RUNDOWN (LRD) - Contains most of the same basic information as the SRD but is set up to allow considerably more space per element to accommodate technical notes. The LRD differs from the SRD in that timing boxes are not used and the LRD seldom appears in the script. It is usually stapled separately and distributed to technical personnel.

SPECIAL NOTE: COMMERCIALS/STATION I.D.'s - Commercial pages which are usually on blue paper, are interspersed throughout the script at each point where a commercial falls. Very little information is needed on the Commercial page. This page states which commercial (1st, 2nd, etc.) and how many minutes must be allotted. Station Identification or Network Promo information is frequently found on the commercial page as these breaks in programming occur at the same time. There might be times when the Station I.D. appears on a separate page following the commercial. In this case the I.D. page might be green. (Writers, while writing to accommodate commercial time, do not include commercial pages in their scripts!)

## CAST AND SET PAGES

### Cast Pages

Different types of shows use different types of Cast and Set pages. The purpose of the cast page in sitcoms and soap operas, for example, is to list all the characters appearing in the script and the names of the persons who will perform the roles. The cast page in other shows such as variety and award shows does not list character roles. Here, the cast page serves more as a contact sheet listing addresses and phone numbers. The need in this case derives from the fact that most of these shows are one-time productions so the personnel are not established.

### Set Pages

As with cast pages, set pages vary for different taped formats. For shows like sitcoms and soap operas, the set page is a list of the set headings in each act.

Variety and award shows do not list sets in this manner. If a specific set is called for, that information appears in the body of the script wherever appropriate.

### Combination Cast/Set Pages

Commonly, cast and set lists are combined on one page. At a glance one sees exactly which characters appear in a given episode and which sets are required. (See Example, page 89)

Note: Filmed series shows may make use of cast and set pages also. Each on a separate page, the format is made up by the production personnel.

### Format: Cast/Set Combined Page

Following is the general format for the combination cast/set pages standard for sitcoms. Other formats for cast and set pages may be determined by production personnel.

The cast is listed first on the page. Both the listing of the cast and the sets should be in capital letters. The heading information will vary with production companies but the usual requirement is the series title, the episode title, and possibly the production number. There is no page number on this page.

Page heading:  EPISODE TITLE - line 4, capitalized and centered.
"Series Title - line 6, upper/lower case in quotes, centered.
Production # - line 8, centered.

Cast listing:  <u>CAST</u> - 4 lines down from last line of heading information, capitalized, underlined, centered.

CHARACTER - Margin (11), capitalized.
ACTOR or ACTRESS - this tab is determined by choosing the longest name and backspacing that many letters from the right margin (76).  Set tab at that point which will usually be (56-61).  (The end of the longest name should leave a little over an inch margin on the right.)

DOTS - are used single or double spaced between the role and the actor/actress playing the role.  The dots should line up vertically on the page.

DOUBLE SPACE down between each character listing.

(See Example 89A, opposite)

Set listing:  <u>SETS</u> - 4 lines down from last cast name, capitalized, underlined, centered.
<u>ACT ONE</u> - double spaced down at margin (11), capitalized and underlined.
FIRST SET HEADING - double spaced down, at margin, capitalized.

Continue to list the sets (and acts) in this fashion double spacing between each and stating the set in the same format as it appears in the script.  (See Example 89B, opposite)

<u>Note</u>:  Some juggling in the space between the cast listing and the set listing is permitted, particularly if this is a long page.

89A - Cast

RUTH'S

"Dinner at Ruth's"

Prod. #32

CAST

RUTH .............................. RUTH CASILOTTI

LANDLORD .......................... ROLAND SMITH

COOKIE ............................ JAMES GREENE

MR. JAMES ......................... GEORGE JOHNSON

PAM ............................... JENNIFER WILLIAMSON

ELIZABETH ......................... STEPHANIE ANDERSON


89B - Sets

SETS

ACT ONE

INT. KITCHEN - MORNING

INT. ANTEROOM - DAY (9:00 A.M.)

INT. LIVING ROOM - MORNING - CONTINUOUS ACTION


ACT TWO

INT. ANTEROOM - MORNING

INT. LIVING ROOM - DAY

INT. KITCHEN - DAY


TAG

INT. KITCHEN - MORNING

# CONTACT LISTS

Special productions like variety, award and special shows have no permanent cast, production crew, sets or locations. Everyone is brought together for the one production and disbanded afterwards. The contact list will include nearly everyone having something to do with the show. This list might be broken down more specifically into CAST LIST, STAFF LIST, CREW LIST, or combinations such as STAFF/CREW LIST. The important thing to remember is that the information must be accurate and easy to read.

Format
    Tabs (7, 31, 61, 73)

    These tabs work as a basic format. Occasionally some juggling must be done to allow for long or additional information.

    First Page:  Heading Information

The heading information on the first page varies according to production company but all require the following:

    Page number - line 4
    TITLE OF SHOW - line 4, centered, capitalized in quotes
    CONTACT LIST (STAFF/CREW LIST) - line 6, centered, capitalized
    DATE - line 7, centered, upper/lower case
    PRODUCTION COMPANY - Margin (7), capitalized
    Address/Phone # - single spaced under, upper/lower case
    NAME OF STUDIO - Tab (56), capitalized
    Address/Phone # - single spaced under, upper/lower case.
        Note: If this information is especially long, move the
        whole block to the left with enough spaces to accommodate.

Second Page:  Heading Information (See example page 92)

Body of List:  Same for first page and those following

The heading information is separated from the body of the list by setting up categories headed: TITLE, NAME & ADDRESS, and PHONE # which appear between solid lines at the above tabs as headers for all pages of the contact list. Body information is single spaced with double spacing used to separate clumps of information.

TITLE (OF PERSON) Margin (7), double spaced down from headings,
        OR            capitalized. If TITLE or SERVICE is too long,
NAME OF SERVICE - form a second line indented 3 spaces.

NAME & ADDRESS   - Tab (31), name capitalized, address upper/lower
                   case, double space to next entry.

PHONE  NUMBER    Tab (61) Differentiate office # by (O) and
                 home/residence # by using (H) or (R) following
                 the number. Phone extension numbers designated
                 with an "X" follow the phone number. When an
                 area code is used in the original phone number
                 leaving no space for the extension, it may be
                 placed on the next line indented 3 spaces.

"TONY OBLEDO'S FIRST SPECIAL"

STAFF LIST

October 5, 1978

RAINBOW PRODUCTIONS
Suite #6790
9000 Sunset Blvd.
Los Angeles, CA 90069
(213) 466-0818

NBC-TV
Stage #2
300 W. Alameda Blvd.
Burbank, CA 91523
(213) 845-7000

| TITLE | NAME & ADDRESS | PHONE # |
|---|---|---|
| EXECUTIVE PRODUCER | RAINBOW PRODUCTIONS<br>Suite #6790<br>9000 Sunset Blvd.<br>Los Angeles, CA 90069 | 723-0901 |
| PRODUCER | B.G. JOHANNESSON<br>1734 Wayland Dr.<br>Beverly Hills, CA 90212 | 725-7425 (O)<br>896-4213 (R) |
| DIRECTOR | BOB NYE<br>Junko Productions<br>6225 W. Olive Ave.<br>Burbank, CA 91505 | 438-4731 (O)<br>438-7000 X2311 (O)<br>721-4165 (R) |
| WRITERS | DOTTIE PEARSON<br>5346 Gayley Ave. #7<br>Los Angeles, CA 90024 | 477-0682 (R) |
|  | BOB LARKIN<br>13742 Valle Dr.<br>Burbank, CA 91505 | 821-1536 (R) |
| MUSICAL DIRECTOR | LOUIS COLE<br>321 Maple Ave.<br>Westwood, CA 90025 | (805)<br>488-7215 X2381 (O)<br>or X2382 |
| ASST. TO THE<br>EXECUTIVE PRODUCER | PATRICIA MORENO<br>1420 N. Mansfield Ave.<br>Hollywood, CA 90028 | 465-0047 (R) |
| REHEARSAL PIANIST<br>REHEARSAL DRUMMER | KEN WERTZ<br>BOB GATES | 836-2744<br>763-4435 |
| PUBLICITY | GORDON BROOKS<br>3814 Cherokee Ave.<br>Hollywood, CA 90028 | 467-4870 |
| INSURANCE | ARTHUR DIXON<br>341 W. 6th St.<br>Los Angeles, CA 90024 | 933-2777 (O) |

"TONY OBLEDO'S FIRST SPECIAL" - STAFF LIST (CONT'D)                    2.

| TITLE | NAME & ADDRESS | PHONE # |
|-------|----------------|---------|
| PRODUCTION ASSISTANT | FRANKIE SCHWARTZ<br>712 Silent Lane<br>Van Nuys, CA 91523 | 555-7777 |

SCHEDULES:   SITCOMS

Preliminaries

The schedules for half hour sitcoms are relatively simple and more
often than not a combination of REHEARSAL/BLOCKING/TAPING.   The
basic information is the same though:  Days, Dates, Times, Places.


Format

   Tabs (11, 51, 73)

   Heading Information

      Page number (or letter) - line 4 (No page number or letter
            used if just one page schedule)

      TITLE OF SERIES - line 4, centered, capitalized, underlined.

      REHEARSAL SCHEDULE (or BLOCKING or TAPING) - line 6, centered,
            capitalized, underlined.

      "Episode Title" - line 8, centered, upper/lower case, in
            quotes.

   Episode Number or Production Number - line 10, centered.

Note:   The heading information varies from show to show, therefore,
the format must sometimes be modified.

Body - Left Column - Margin (11)

   DAY/DATE - line 12, capitalized, underlined, single spaced to
            form a heading.
   TIME - always stipulates A.M. or P.M.  Must be set up so that
            colons separating the numbers and the hyphens
            separating the times are vertically lined up.  (See
            Example 94A, opposite)

Body - Right column - Tab (51)

   STAGE (or AREA) - capitalized, underlined to form a heading.

   ACTIVITY (READING, RUN THRU, ETC.) - capitalized, single
            spaced.  Must appear directly across from the time it
            takes place.  May appear upper/lower case with
            capitalization used to spotlight some entries.  When
            capitalized, underling is used to spotlight.  (See
            Example 94B, opposite)

## EXAMPLE: REHEARSAL/TAPE SCHEDULES - SITCOMS

### RUTH'S

### REHEARSAL/TAPE SCHEDULE

"Dinner at Ruth's"

| 94A - Date/Time | 94B - Place/Activity |
|---|---|

42-09-RUTH-81

**MONDAY, MARCH 16, 1981**                    STAGE 57, ABC

 9:30A - 12:30P          READING & REHEARSAL
12:30P -  1:30P          LUNCH
 1:30P -  4:30P          REHEARSAL


**TUESDAY, MARCH 17, 1981**

 9:30A - 12:30P          REHEARSAL
12:30P -  1:30P          LUNCH
 1:30P -  4:00P          REHEARSAL
 4:00P -  6:00P          RUN-THRU
 6:00P -                 NOTES/REWRITE


**WEDNESDAY, MARCH 18, 1981**

 9:30A - 12:30P          REHEARSAL
12:30P -  1:30P          LUNCH
 1:30P -  4:00P          REHEARSAL/BLOCKING
 4:00P -  6:00P          RUN-THRU


**THURSDAY, MARCH 19, 1981**

 9:30A - 12:30P          REHEARSAL/BLOCKING
12:30P -  1:30P          LUNCH
 1:30P -  4:00P          REHEARSAL/BLOCKING


**FRIDAY, MARCH 20, 1981**                    STUDIO B, ABC

12:00N - 12:30P          MAKEUP & HAIR
12:30P -  1:30P          ESU
 1:30P -  5:30P          BLOCK & TAPE (DRESS)
 5:30P -  6:30P          MEAL
 6:30P -  7:00P          NOTES/AUDIENCE IN
 7:00P -  7:30P          WARM-UP
 7:30P -  9:00P          VTR (AIR) W/AUDIENCE

## Preliminaries

Like any other schedule of activities, these schedules serve to
designate those times and places where performers and production
personnel are to appear for the rehearsing, blocking and taping of
specific segments of the show.  Content of these schedules is
consistent in that they all list dates, times, places, segments or
musical numbers, and relevant cast along with the script page number
where the material may be found.

Frequently, rehearsal and blocking are done at the same time; hence,
the schedules are combined.

## Format

The format for schedules is the same for all pages.  Headings remain
the same also with the exception of the day and date.  If one day's
schedule requires two pages, (CONT'D) is added after the date.

Note:  Schedule pages are numbered consecutively when the schedule
is such that each day is on a single page.  If each day's schedule
requires more than one page, say two or three, each day is itself
numbered consecutively.

    Tabs (7, 26, 31, 61, 73)

## Heading Information

The heading information on schedules is usually no more than a
couple of lines long, separated from the body of the schedule by
a double solid line, running margin to margin.  Some or all of
the following information is included depending on the
requirements of the production company.

    Line 3:
        Begin at margin (7) and continue across the page with:
        1)   REHEARSAL SCHEDULE (or BLOCKING/TAPING SCHEDULE,
        etc.)  2)  DAY and DATE  3)  SHOW TITLE

    Line 4:
        Begin back at margin and again continue across the page
        with:   1)   PLACE OF REHEARSAL   2)   ADDRESS   3)   PHONE
        NUMBER and whatever additional information is requested.
        Note:  Remember that the page number must be on tab (73).

    Double Solid Lines...
        margin to margin are used under the last line of
        information to separate it from the body of the schedule.

<u>Note</u>:   Columns May Have Headings

    If there are column headings (See example page 97, column titled
    AREA) they should be double spaced down from the double line
    separating the heading from the body and placed above the
    appropriate column.

## Body of the Schedule

    First Column - Time:
    Margin (7), must indicate A.M. or P.M. or simply A. or P.  Colons
    between the numbers must line up vertically.  Hyphens between
    each time indication must also line up vertically.

    Second Column - Script Page Number Where Item Begins:
    tab (26), on the same line as time, in parentheses.  The
    parentheses must line up vertically down the page.  To allow for
    double digit page numbers (or triple in some cases) leave one
    space (or two) inside the parentheses.

    Third Column:
    Segment - Tab (31), capitalized
    Cast - Single spaced below, upper/lower case, in parentheses.
    <u>Note</u>:   (To technicians, if used), single spaced down,
    capitalized, with underlining optional.

------------------------------------------------------------------

## LUNCH BREAKS

    are designated between broken lines, margin to margin.

------------------------------------------------------------------

## INDIVIDUAL CALL TIMES...

    are listed after the last time designation for the day's
    schedule.  This category is separated from the body of the script
    with a solid line, margin to margin.

    <u>Format Note</u>:  The format for individual calls involves only one
                  time indication, the name of the person, and what
                  activity he is being called for... Makeup,
                  Wardrobe, etc.  Other information may appear, for
                  example, instructions for special equipment.

(See Schedule example on following pages)

| Time | | Segment | Area |
|------|---|---------|------|
| 11:00A - 12:00N | | DRY BLOCK IN FULL COSTUME | AREA |
| | ( 4) | BOYFRIEND | STG RT |
| | | (Richard, Beverly, James, Jennifer) | |
| | | NOTE:  MARK IN FULL MAKEUP | |
| 12:00N - 12:30P | (29) | WATERDROPPINGS | STG L |
| | | (Beverly, John, Jennifer, Richard, Melanie) | |
| 12:30P - 1:30P | (58) | MACHO | STG L |
| | | (James, Richard, Harry, John, Beverly, Melanie) | |
| 1:30P - 2:15P | (38) | AHH KEE BOH! | STG L |
| | | (Harry, Beverly, Richard, John) | |
| 2:15P - 3:00P | (72) | CPA GROUPIES | STG L |
| | | (Beverly, Melanie, Jennifer, John, Richard, James) | |
| 3:00P - 3:30P | (14) | FRIDAY EDITION | BANDSTAND |
| | | (John, Melanie) | & STG L |
| | | NOTE:  JOHN IN FULL MAKEUP | |

---

| Time | Segment | Area |
|------|---------|------|
| 3:30P - 4:30P | LUNCH | |

---

| Time | | Segment | Area |
|------|---|---------|------|
| 4:30P - 5:30P | | AUDIO BALANCE: | |
| | | HOUSE BAND | BANDSTAND |
| | | (House Band) | |
| 5:30P - 7:30P | | AUDIO BALANCE & DRY BLOCK: | |
| | (23) | "KEEP THE FIRE" | STG R |
| | | (Steve Smith) | |
| | (46) | "THIS IS IT" | AUDIO NOTE: |
| | | (Steve Smith) | MAKE 2 AUDIO |
| | | | CASSETTES OF |
| | | | REHEARSAL |

## INDIVIDUAL CALL TIMES:

|  |  |  |  |
|------|--------|------|------|
| 10:00A | JAMES (MAKE-UP) | 12:30P | JOHN TO MAKE-UP |
| 10:30A | RICHARD BEVERLY JENNIFER | 3:30P | MOVE STEVE SMITH EQUIPMENT FROM R.H. #1 TO STUDIO 55 & SET FOR REHEARSAL |
| 11:30A | JOHN MELANIE JAMES | 4:30P | HOUSE BAND READY TO PLAY |
| | | 5:15P | STEVE SMITH BAND |
| 12:00N | HARRY | | |

| | | | | |
|---|---|---|---|---|
| 4:00P - 4:30P | (70) | GOODNIGHTS (Full Cast) | | BACK ROOM |
| 4:30P - 5:30P | (72) | C.P.A. GROUPIES (Beverly, Melanie, Jennifer, John, Harry, Richard) | | STG L |

-----------------------------------------------------------------

5:30P - 6:15P         DINNER

-----------------------------------------------------------------

| | | | |
|---|---|---|---|
| 6:15P - 6:45P | | ESU | |
| 6:15P - 8:30P | | RE-BALANCE & BLOCK: | |
| | (23) | "KEEP THE FIRE" (Steve Smith) | STG RT |
| | (46) | "THIS IS IT" (Steve Smith) | STG RT |
| 6:45P - 7:15P | | VTR: POLAROIDS FOR CLOSING CREDITS | CHYRON PB |
| | | GRAPHICS | |

INDIVIDUAL CALL TIMES:  TBA

Preliminaries

The short rundown is a listing of all the various segments in the show including musical numbers and commercials. It serves two purposes. It is a timing sheet, its main purpose. It also acts as a table of contents for the script, each item referenced with a page number in the script. The SRD is easily distinguishable from other special pages in the script since it employs boxes for each segment where timings are recorded. The production personnel decides how many boxes are needed.

Segments are numbered consecutively at the margin. These numbers are called ITEM numbers. Item numbers must appear at the top of the script pages.

Short rundowns are sometimes used for sitcoms and follow the basic format considerations. In this case there will probably be no more than four boxes for timings as opposed to five or even six in a variety or awards show. The SRD in a sitcom will probably be less than two pages. (See Example, Page 101)

Format

Tabs (7, 12, 38, 73)

Heading Information

The amount and type of information varies according to production company. The following entries, however, are always necessary.

Line 3, Heading:
Begin at left margin (7) and continue across the page with: 1) TITLE OF SHOW, capitalized, in quotes 2) SHORT RUNDOWN (if it fits, otherwise next line) 3) VTR: date. Separate items using dashes with spaces on either side. A production number may or may not be used.
Line 4, Heading (2nd line):
Begin back at left margin again, single spaced down and continue across the page with: 1) SHORT RUNDOWN (if it didn't fit on line 3. 2) AIR: date positioned under VTR: date, and finally page number.
Double Solid Lines:
are used to separate this heading information from the body of the page. These appear directly under the last entry of the heading, running from margin to margin.

Succeeding Page Heading:
Headings on succeeding pages of the SRD differ in that the word (CONT'D) must be used after SHORT RUNDOWN. (See example, page 103)

Sometimes in the case of exceptionally long heading information, the information is reduced on succeeding pages to 1) TITLE OF SHOW, 2) SHORT RUNDOWN (CONT'D).

The Body of the Short Rundown:
Same for all pages. Each segment along with the cast of that segment is listed down the left side of the page, numbered consecutively and separated by solid lines running from margin to margin. Act designations may also be included. Format rules are as follows:

Item Number:
Margin (7) followed by a period.
Segment (or Opening or Commercial or Promo):
Tab (12) on same line as item number, capitalized, underlined. If the segment title is unusually long, it must continue on the next line, single spaced, at tab (12) so that it doesn't run into the page number.
Script Page Number Where the Segment Begins:
Tab (38). The number is enclosed in parentheses. The parentheses must line up vertically down the page for all segments. To allow for double digit page numbers (or triple if that is the case) leave one space (or two) inside the parentheses.
Segment Cast Listing:
Tab (12), upper/lower case, enclosed in parentheses with names separated by commas. If the cast list extends to the next line, single space down and begin on tab (13), one space in. Do not go past the end parenthesis of the Script Page Number.
A Solid Line...
is placed from margin to margin under the last entry.

Rule: If the entry is only two lines of information then the solid line must be single spaced down to allow at least three lines per each segment. This allows sufficient space for the Production Assistant to write in the timing.
Vertical Lines...
must be drawn to provide the desired number of boxes. The number of boxes may vary from three to even six or more.

Page 2, heading information (See example, page 103).

"JUDY AND THE FARM" - FINAL DRAFT - SHORT RUNDOWN          DATE _____

VTR:  9/22/88

| | | | | |
|---|---|---|---|---|
| ACT ONE - Scene 1                    ( 1)<br>STOCK SHOT - EXT. HOUSE - DAY<br>INT. KITCHEN/LIVING ROOM/HALLWAY/<br>EXAMINING ROOM/WAITING ROOM<br><br>(Judy, Dick, Greg, Glenda,<br>(Bossy, Cows, Extras) | | | | |
| ACT ONE - Scene 2                    (10)<br>INT. HALLWAY/LIVING ROOM -<br>SAME DAY - CONTINUOUS ACTION<br><br>(Judy, Dick, Nancy) | | | | |
| ACT ONE - Scene 3-6                  (12)<br>INT. EXAMINING ROOM/HALLWAY/<br>LIVING ROOM - SAME DAY -<br>CONTINUOUS ACTION<br><br>(Greg, Bossy, Nancy, Judy,<br>Dick, Glenda, Sean) | | | | |
| ACT TWO, Scene 1                     (24)<br>INT. EXAMINING ROOM - SAME DAY<br><br>(Glenda, Greg, Polly, Maisie) | | | | |
| ACT TWO, Scene 2-3                   (28)<br>INT. LIVING ROOM/KITCHEN - NIGHT<br>SAME DAY<br><br>(Judy, Dick) | | | | |
| ACT TWO, Scene 4-7                   (30)<br>INT. WAITING ROOM - SAME NIGHT<br><br>(Greg, Glenda, Maisie) | | | | |

| "MOUNTAIN HOLIDAY"<br>SHORT RUNDOWN | | | VTR:  9/3,4,5/88<br>AIR:  12/22/88 8-9:00P | | | 1. |
|---|---|---|---|---|---|---|
| 1. | OPENING TEASES<br>(Dick, Roberta) | ( 1) | | | | |
| 2. | A.   INTRO MOUNTAIN TOP<br>      (Dick, Roberta) | ( 5) | | | | |
| | B.   MOUNTAIN TOP SATELLITE<br>      INTERVIEW<br>      (Dick, Roberta, Jeremy<br>      Greene, Steve Sato) | ( 6) | | | | |
| | C.   MOUNTAIN TOP CLIP<br>      (VTPB) | ( 7) | | | | |
| 3. | COMMERCIAL #1 | ( 8) | 1:02 | | | |
| 4. | A.   SLEIGH RACE INTRO<br>      (Dick, Roberta) | ( 9) | | | | |
| | B.   SLEIGH RACE CLIP<br>      (VTPB) | (10) | | | | |
| 5. | TEASES INTO COMMERCIAL #2<br>(Dick, Roberta) | (16) | | | | |
| 6. | ABC ID BUMPER | (17) | :05 | | | |
| 7. | COMMERCIAL #2 | (18) | 1:32 | | | |
| 8. | A.   INTRO REINDEER, PT.1<br>      (Dick, Roberta) | (19) | | | | |
| | B.   REINDEER CLIP/PT.1<br>      (VTPB) | (20) | | | | |
| | E.   REINDEER TAG<br>      (Dick, Roberta, Sean,<br>      Steve Olsen, Richard<br>      Miller) | (24) | | | | |
| 9. | TEASES INTO COMMERCIAL #3<br>(Dick) | (25) | | | | |
| 10. | COMMERCIAL #3 | (26) | 1:02 | | | |

| "MOUNTAIN HOLIDAY" SHORT RUNDOWN (CONT'D) | | VTR: 9/3,4,5/88 AIR: 12/22/88 8-9:00P | | | 2. |
|---|---|---|---|---|---|
| 11. BUMPER<br>------<br>MID-NET IDENT/<br>MID-STATION BREAK<br>------<br>BUMPER MUSIC OVER | (27) | | | | |
| 12. A.   INTRO WINTER PRINCESS<br>CASTLE<br>(Dick) | (28) | | | | |
| B.   WINTER PRINCESS CASTLE<br>CLIP<br>(VTPB) (V.O.'S) | (29) | | | | |
| C.   WINTER PRINCESS CASTLE<br>TAG<br>(Dick) | (30) | | | | |
| 13. D.   INTRO WINTER PRINCESS<br>BOAT<br>(Dick) | (31) | | | | |
| E.   WINTER PRINCESS BOAT<br>CLIP<br>(VTPB) | (32) | | | | |
| 14. TEASES INTO COMMERCIAL #4<br>(Dick) | (33) | | | | |
| 15. COMMERCIAL #4<br>------<br>ABC PROMO | (34) | 1:32<br>:31 | | | |
| 16. A.   ICE MAN<br>(Dick, Michael Allen) | (43) | | | | |
| 17. BUMPER | (46) | :05 | | | |
| 18. COMMERCIAL #5 | (47) | 1:02 | | | |
| 19. GOODNIGHTS/CLOSING<br>TEASES<br>(Dick, Roberta) | (48) | | | | |
| 20. CLOSING CREDITS | (51) | | | | |

LONG RUNDOWNS

Preliminaries

The long rundown (LRD) contains the same basic information as the short rundown (SRD) except that considerably more space is allotted for each item and boxes are not used. Horizontal lines separate each item with as few a two or three items appearing on each page. These large spaces are utilized by certain technical personnel for notes.

Information appearing on the long rundown, like the short rundown is 1) the chronological item numbering of segments which corresponds with the SRD  2) the segment  3) the cast  4) the script page number reference. (Commercials, promo's and network I.D.'s are included but occupy far less space)

Format

    Tabs (11, 16, 69, 73)

    Heading Information:  First Page

        Line 4:
            TITLE OF SHOW, capitalized at margin (11)
            LONG RUN capitalized and placed 4 or 5 spaces over from title (depending on title length)
            AIR DATE, capitalized and placed 4 or 5 spaces over from LONG RUNDOWN
            PAGE NUMBER, TAB (73)

            Note:  It's important that heading information remains uncrowded and easy to read.  A second line may be used if necessary.

            Double solid lines are used to separate the heading from the body.

    Heading Information:  Subsequent Pages...
        ... may be shortened to:  SHOW TITLE, LONG RUNDOWN (CONT'D), and the date.

    Body (Double spaced down from the double solid lines)

        Line 8:
            Number 1. (always followed by a period) at Tab (11)
            SEGMENT, capitalized, underlined at Tab (16)
            Page number in script, isolated in parentheses at Tab (69)

        Line 9:
            Cast listing, upper/lower case at Tab (16)    (The cast listing should cut off at the center of the page)

Long rundown examples are found on pages 105 and 106.

"OPENING NIGHT" - LONG RUNDOWN - SATURDAY, OCTOBER 14, 1978          1.

1.  SKETCH:  DANCE LESSON                                          (39)
    (Henry Hanes, John Powell,
    Edith Bell)

_____

2.  JUSTICE BY THE NUMBERS                                         (12)
    (Henry Hanes, Miranda, John
    Powell, Sandy Bonner)

_____

3.  HENRY HANES MONOLOGUE                                          (46)
    (Henry Hanes)

"OPENING NIGHT" - LONG RUNDOWN (CONT'D) - SATURDAY, 10/14/78         2.

4.  MIRANDA'S DANCE                                               (17)
    (Miranda, her 4 dancers)




5.  INTERMISSION - LOBBY CAMEOS                                   (20)
    (Gary Langdon, Bob Cairo, Greg Coogan,
    Jimmy Jones, Carmen de Carlo, Mark
    Donahue, Harold Ray, Nina Nelson,
    Virginia Smith, Bob Dugan, Brigette
    Brown)




6.  INTERMISSION SKETCH                                           (28)
    A)  LOBBY
    (Gary Langdon, Bob Cairo, John
    Powell, Sean MacGregor)

COMMERCIAL PAGES

Preliminaries

Commercial pages list the commercial (and the commercial sequence
number), promo, station identification and various other information
when needed along with the timings for each on the same page.  Each
commercial is numbered. (See example opposite)  Commercial pages are
numbered within the chronological page sequence of the script.

Occasionally, the commercials will appear on separate pages.  The
same format is used.

Blue for Commercials

Commercial pages are run on blue paper to easily set them apart from
the white body of the script.

INTO:

What may also appear on the commercial page near the bottom on line
57 or 58 is an INTO: slug stating which segment is next.  (See
example opposite)

Format
(Some or all of the following may be listed)

    ITEM NUMBER
        Line 4, capitalized, underlined, centered.
    PAGE NUMBER
        Line 4 at tab (73)
    COMMERCIAL NUMBER AND TIMING
        Line 6, capitalized, underlined, centered, backspaced from the
        period of the page number.
    PROMO AND TIMING
        Line 7, capitalized, underlined, positioned directly under the
        "C" of COMMERCIAL.  (Set a tab here)
    STATION BREAK AND TIMING
        Line 8, capitalized, underlined, same as tab set above.
    TITLE ART WORK
        Line 9, capitalized, underlined, same as tab above.
    BUMPER AND TIMING
        Line 10, capitalized, underlined, same tab as above.

ITEM #17                                        31.

COMMERCIAL #2 (2:02)
PROMO         ( :07)
STATION BREAK (1:55)
TITLE ART WORK
BUMPER        ( :07)

(INTO:  INDIAN SKIT)

ITEM #18                                    16.

COMMERCIAL #2 (2:00)

(INTO:  FISHERMAN SKIT)

VARIETY, AWARD, AND SPECIAL SHOWS

Main Body of the Script

Preliminaries

Variety shows, specials, and award shows tend to fall into the same
category not only because they all employ Tape-Live Format but
because of the similar myriad details that must be incorporated into
that format.  These shows usually involve a large cast, elaborate
sets and costumes, musicians, singers, dancers, and the like.  This
means that more information will be necessary in the script.  The
content is divided into segments:  a skit, a song, an award, a commercial, presentation of an award, acceptance, etc.  Each page
displays a segment slug indicating the segment title, and on the
first page of the segment, the segment cast list.  Item numbers are
also used.  Occasionally technical information such as props, sets,
light cues, etc., are listed down the right side of the page.  These
details along with methods of handling music and lyrics contribute
to the script's complexities.

Format:  Segment Beginnings

All the basic rules discussed for Tape-Live Format in this volume
generally apply.  Our discussion here will focus on those additional
elements -- segment slugs, cast lists, technical notations -- that
are an overlay to this Tape-Live Script form.  The basic unit of
these shows is the segment.  For that reason we begin with handling
segments.

   Tabs (11, 16, 31, 73)

   On the First Page of Each Segment:
      Page number:
         Line 4, centered, capitalized OR directly above the segment
         slug, capitalized and underlined.
      Segment Slug:
         Line 6, backspaced from the right margin (76), in capital
         letters, underlined.

         Note:  Remember that the length of this line dictates the
         amount of space available for the cast listing.  Therefore,
         if the segment slug is very short (Example:  OPENING) it
         might be necessary to move the segment slug farther to the
         left to accommodate at least one full cast name per line.
         (See Example 110A, following)  If the segment slug is
         unusually long, it must be broken appropriately and single
         spaced down to form a second line.  (See Example 110B,
         following)

      Segment Cast List:
         Single spaced under the segment slug in upper/lower case,
         enclosed in parentheses.

         Note:  When the cast list extends onto two lines, the
         second line is indented one space under the first letter of
         the first name.  (See Example 110B, following)

Format (Cont'd)

Special Technical Notations:
SET: PROPS: LITE Q: SPFX: sometimes appear in a separate listing at the right side of the page. Tab (61). Each of these headings appears capitalized, and underlined, followed by a colon. The entries are then listed under the appropriate headings in upper/lower, singled spaced and abbreviated where possible to accommodate space available. SET: is the first listing and appears directly across from the line of direction introducing the segment and 4 lines down from the last line of cast. The other headings appear in the same format with double spacing used to separate each package of information. (See example opposite)
Note: Sometimes PROPS:, LITE Q:, SPFX:, etc., might be slugged across from the specific direction or dialogue where the cue is called for.

Body of the Page...
... begins 4 lines down from the last line of cast listing. (On subsequent pages of the segment, the body begins only 2 lines down from the slug (CONT'D). The body may begin with a character cue and dialogue introducing a person or skit, or direction leading into a skit, or a music cue leading into a song. (See example, page 112) The stage direction, personal direction, character cues and dialogue are handled according to all the same rules and considerations discussed in the section on Tape-Live Format.

Character Cue - Tab (31), capitalized.
Dialogue      Tab (16), upper/lower case, double spaced. Cut off (51).
Direction    - Margin (11), capitalized, single spaced, in parentheses. Cut off (46). When paragraphing is used, each paragraph is enclosed in its own set of parentheses.

Note: Sketches are "10 minute sitcoms" in that the characters are stereotyped and their vehicle is situation.

110A

ITEM #2                                                    4.

FRIDAY EDITION:  RILEY DAVIS
INTERVIEW
(John, Melanie)

------------------------------------------------------------

110B - Two Line Cast List

                                                           2.

ITEM #1
OPENING
(Jennifer, Michael,
Richard)

        SET:  DRESSING ROOM

        PROPS:  Make-up,
                Wigs

        LITE Q:  DIM LITES

VARIETY, AWARD, AND SPECIAL SHOWS

Format (Cont'd)

On the Second Page...

... the cast is not listed under the segment slug.  Instead
the word (CONT'D) appears.

The body of the script begins <u>two lines</u> down from (CONT'D)
beneath the segment slug.  (See example on page opposite)

<u>Note</u>:  (MORE) is used <u>only</u> when the dialogue or music lyrics
of a specific artist continue from one page to the next.  At
the bottom of the page, (MORE) is double spaced down from the
script body (dialogue or lyrics) and is placed on the
character cue tab.  On the top of the next page (CONT'D) must
appear next to the character name.  This particular (CONT'D)
applies only to the character.  There will be another (CONT'D)
under the segment slug to indicate that the segment continues
as well.

3.

OPENING
(CONT'D)

(MELANIE GOES CRAZY AND JUMPS
UP AND DOWN)

                    MARY

What's the matter with her?

## MUSIC CUES

### Preliminaries

Invariably variety and award shows and specials will utilize
music. When the orchestra plays a few short bars to introduce a
performer to "play" him/her onto the stage this is indicated in the
script as MUSIC: PLAYON. MUSIC: PLAYOFF is used when he or she
exits. Any time music is used as part of the show it is indicated
in the script. When a performer sings, the music cue will
incorporate the title of the song in quotes thusly:

MUSIC: "ALL ALONE"

Other notations may appear in conjunction with a music cue. (TRACK)
or (TT) meaning TOTAL TRACK indicates that the music and lyrics have
been pre-recorded and the performer will simply mouth (lip sinc) the
words. (A/T), (LIVE), or time (:32) may also appear. These
notations follow the music cue and are placed in parentheses. The
music cue itself requires a broken underline and appears isolated at
the margin (16) working as stage direction. The accompanying
notations are not underlined.

### Format

Music cues appear at the left margin tab (16), capitalized, followed
by a colon and underscored with a broken underline. (See example
opposite)

MUSIC: "AS TIME GOES BY" (TT) (1:30)

MUSIC: PLAYON "AWARD THEME SONG"

MUSIC: JOHNNY/BARBARA MEDLEY (3:10)

## MUSIC LYRICS

### Preliminaries

The lyrics of a song will always appear in the script even though the performer is mouthing the words (lip sync) to a pre-recorded track. The lyrics are handled in a specific, standard manner.

### Format

#### Performer's Cue

The person or persons singing the song are stated at the character cue tab (31). If two or more persons are singing, slashes are used between the names. Sometimes when a group performs, some of the lyrics are sung by one person in the group and some lyrics are sung by ALL of the group. This must be noted with specific character cues such as CHARLIE, ALL (Charlie being one of the all).

#### Lines of the Lyric

The lyric itself begins at the dialogue tab (16). Frequently, lyric lines extend past the dialogue cut off point. This is acceptable since it is important to keep the line intact. If the line is unusually long then it must be triple spaced down to form a second line, indented three spaces. (See example opposite)

#### Spacing for Lyrics

Lyrics are always triple spaced unless the production company specifically requests double spacing. Four lines are used between verses.

Note: Punctuation is not used in lyrics, not even periods!

#### (MORE) and (CONT'D)

(MORE) and (CONT'D) are used to continue both lyrics and dialogue from one page to the next. These terms are used in exactly the same way as they are used in Tape-Live Format. What must be emphasized is that (MORE) and (CONT'D) are used only to continue a specific artist(s) lyrics or dialogue. Remember: (MORE) and (CONT'D) only have to do with that which comes out of people's mouths, specifically dialogue and lyrics.

MUSIC: ORCHESTRA DOWN BEAT INTO
       VOCAL "CHEATIN' WOMAN" (TT) (1:03)

                JAMES/POLLY/CHARLEY

I'VE NOT HAD ANY REASON TO DOUBT HER

AS FAR AS I KNOW SHE'S BEEN TRUE

BUT LATELY SHE'S HAD A DIFFERENT LOOK

        IN HER EYES

WONDER IF SHE'S SEEING SOMEBODY NEW

              (MORE)

-------------------------- next page ---------------------------

                                                          6.

              JAMES/POLLY/CHARLEY (CONT'D)

MUSIC: KEY CHANGE

   'CAUSE SHE JUST STARTED LIKING CHEATIN' SONGS

   THAT'S WHAT'S BOTHERING ME

   I DON'T KNOW IF IT'S THE CHEATIN' SHE LIKES

   OR JUST THE MELODY

## SIMULTANEOUS LYRICS

### Preliminaries

When simultaneous lyrics occur, tabs must be set to accommodate sets
of lyrics which are being sung at the same time; an artist singing
with a chorus, for example.  The lyrics to be sung together appear
on the left and on the right sides of the page, across from one
another, the parallel lyrics running for the same number of bars.

### Format

    Left side:
        Character Cue, tab (21)
        Lyrics, tab (11), cut off to leave at least five spaces
        between this set of lyrics and the right side set of
        lyrics.

    Right Side:
        Backspace from the right margin (76) the length of the
        longest lyric line.  (This assumes that the longest line
        will not overlap the first lyrics.  A second line may be to
        be formed.)  Set lyric tab.
        Character Cue is spaced in 5 spaces from the lyric tab.

    (See example opposite)

MUSIC:  "WHEN THE RED, RED ROBIN COMES
        BOB, BOB, BOBBING ALONG"

           PERRY                                    CHORUS

WHEN THE RED RED ROBIN                         RED RED ROBIN

COMES BOB BOB BOBBIN'                          BOB BOB BOBBING

ALONG, ALONG

        OOH, AHHH

              (-2-)

## MUSIC BARS

### Preliminaries

Interspersed within the lyrics of a song may be numbers that indicate bars of orchestration. There may also be a designation specifying what those bars are to be -- INSTRUMENTAL, GUITAR, VAMP, etc. The numbers may also indicate that DANCE will be taking place.

### Format

The figure which indicates the number of bars to be played should appear triple spaced down from the last line of lyric on tab (56), the character cue tab. The number will employ a hyphen on either side and will probably be placed in parentheses. (Parentheses are optional.) The important format consideration is that the number of bars indicated dictates the number of lines which must be spaced down the page after the number is stated. If there are (-6-) bars, then space down six spaces to the next line of lyric or whatever comes next... it may be more bars. If there are (-12-) bars, space down 12 lines, and so on.

(See example opposite)

MUSIC:  "JINGLE, JANGLE, JINGLE"  (TRACK)

(-6-) VAMP

(-8-) SPANISH STYLE

LINDA

SPURS THAT JINGLE, JANGLE, JINGLE

AS I GO RIDIN' ON MY MERRY WAY

(-12-) DANCE

LINDA

SPURS THAT JINGLE, JANGLE, JINGLE

AS I GO RIDIN' ON MY MERRY WAY

<u>STOP TAPE AND INTO:</u>

STOP TAPE

STOP TAPE is a term occasionally used at the end of a segment.  It should appear on line 56.  A solid line begins at the left margin with the words STOP TAPE at tab (56).  After the STOP TAPE is stated the solid line extends to the right margin (76).  It will look like this:

_____STOP TAPE_____


INTO:

INTO: is often used at the end of a segment to indicate the next segment.  INTO: appears on line 58 at the margin (11) in parentheses, capitalized and punctuated with a colon.

(INTO:  CARMEN SPOT)


        OR


(INTO:  "SINGIN' IN THE RAIN")


The following several pages make up a segment of a variety show.  Most of the information previously discussed is represented.

ITEM #5
COMICS MEET
(Ann, Mike)


MUSIC: STRIP MUSIC (TT) (:10)

(-8-)


(ANN, SEXILY ATTIRED, DANCES ON
STAGE, BUMPS AND GRINDS FROM
AISLE. MIKE BLOWS A WHISTLE AND
RUNS ONSTAGE)

MUSIC: OUT

MIKE

(TO AUDIENCE)

Everybody go home. I'm closing the

show. Everybody go home.

ANN

(INTERRUPTING)

Just a minute, just a minute. Just

who do you think you are -- running

down this aisle, saying everybody go

home, that you're closing the

show. Just who do you think you

are? I want to talk about Mexico.

(MORE)

ANN (CONT'D)

I love Mexico.  I go there all the
time.  Oh, that new bullfighter.

MIKE

Oh, what's his name.  Enchilada?
Oh, yeah, he's wonderful.  Would you
like to see him again?

ANN

Oh, I would.

MIKE

Get a shovel, he's dead.  Oh, yeah.

ANN

What happened?

MIKE

Well, you know what a crazy
bullfight it was.  The truth.  When
he killed the bull, he cut him up
and then he would eat him and then
he would sing.  Well, somebody heard
him singing and they shot him.  They
did.

ANN

Noooo!

MIKE

Yeah.  And the moral of the story

is, when you're full of bull, keep

your mouth shut.

MUSIC:  PLAYOFF

(INTO:  ITEM #6/"ROSEY APPLE")

## 21

MUSIC:  "ROSEY APPLE"

                    (-1-) INTRO

                GIRLS

DA DA DA DA DA DA

OOH MAY I TEMPT YOU WITH

A BIG RED ROSEY APPLE

                    ANN

HEY THERE BIG BOY

HOW'S ABOUT A BITE

                GIRLS

MAY I TEMPT YOU WITH

A BIG RED ROSEY APPLE

                    ANN

LET ME BE YOUR PIPPIN FOR TONIGHT

WE'LL BE TRUE

WE'LL NEVER BE MISLEADIN'

                (MORE)

## 22

ANN (CONT'D)

WE CAN BE LIKE ADAM AND EVE

WALKIN' IN THE GARDEN OF EDEN

MAY I TEMPT YOU WITH

MY BIG RED ROSEY APPLE

'CAUSE YOU'RE THE APPLE OF MY EYE

OH MY YOU'RE THE APPLE OF MY EYE

(-4-) DRUMS

(REPRISE)          ANN/GIRLS

WE'LL BE TRUE

WE'LL NEVER BE MISLEADIN'

WE CAN BE LIKE ADAM AND EVE

WALKIN' IN THE GARDEN OF EDEN

MAY I TEMPT YOU WITH

A BIG RED ROSEY APPLE

'CAUSE YOU'RE THE APPLE OF MY EYE

(INTO:  ITEM #7/MUSIC TEACHER)

## REVISION PAGES

The following section covers revision pages or "change"
pages which is a production consideration.  Writers of
spec scripts are not concerned with revision pages but
rather do re-writes so that a clean script may be
presented.

Preliminaries

Revision pages are an aspect of the production part of a given
script when the production personnel add or delete words, lines,
scenes, and sometimes nearly the whole script it seems. Regardless
of the format of a script, the revision pages are handled according
to the same rules, following the format of the original script.


Color Coding

Revision pages follow a specific color code. This color code
progresses from blue for the first revision, pink, yellow, green,
gold, buff, salmon, cherry, tan and finally back to white. A fully
revised script may be run entirely on a single color.


Always "Hold" Page and Scene Numbers

This means that page and scene numbers must be kept essentially the
"same." They may not be renumbered. This is achieved by indicating
that certain scenes have been omitted or by using "A" scenes for
material added.


What are "A" Pages?

There are times when added material will not fit on a given page and
may extend onto an additional page or pages. In this case "A" pages
are used. The original page number is retained and all subsequent
pages use capital letters along with the page number. The page
numbers then, might run 12., 12A., 12B, 13. An asterisk following
the page number indicates that the page contains at least 2/3 new
material. (See example on page 138)


What are Runs?

If, on the other hand, material is omitted to the extent that two
pages fit on one, or five pages fit on three consecutive pages, this
is referred to as a "run". The pages in question are tightened up
or typed omitting the deleted material and numbered consecutively to
the last page of the run. The last page becomes a combination page
which means that the page contains a combination page number such as
3/4. or 3-5., etc. This last page of the run must flow
chronologically into the next page number of the original script.

REVISION PAGES:  HEADINGS

Headings May Vary According to Production Company

Revision pages must carry an information heading or slug at the top
of each page that is revised.  This slug will most often state the
title of the show and the current date.  It may just use the
abbreviation REV. (for revised) and the date.  In any case, the
current date should always be used in the slug.  This information is
stated on line 4 at margin (11).

Asterisks are used on both individual revised pages and also in revised scripts to indicate the places where material has been changed, added, or deleted.

There are specific rules regarding the use of asterisks.  These rules eliminate an abundance of asterisks cascading down the page, causing needless clutter.

Asterisking Line Changes Only

Specific lines that have been changed are asterisked at tab (76) directly across from the specific line changed.  (See example, page 136)

The 2/3 Rule

    (a)    Asterisk by the Character Cue When...

        ... a character's dialogue has been changed completely or has been at least 2/3 changed.  The asterisk should be placed on the same line as the character cue at tab (76).  (See example, page 137)

    (b)    Asterisk by the Page Number When...

        ... more than 2/3 of a page has been changed.  The asterisk should fall after the period of the page number.  (See example, page 138)

Asterisking Lines or Paragraphs Omitted

When a line or lines have been deleted, and a natural spacing occurs immediate after, the asterisk should appear on the blank line to indicate that something is missing.  (See example, page 138)

The next three pages are composite examples of revision pages.

                    RUTH

Something's really wrong with this adding

machine.  I have to go over these figures

again.  (RIPS OFF TAPE)  Look at this.  I

added forty-seven plus three and came up

with one hundred and five.  *It's all screwed up.*

SFX:  PHONE RINGS

IRVING ENTERS THE OFFICE IN A FLURRY, SITS AT HIS DESK AND
OPENS HIS BRIEFCASE.  SOME PAPERS FALL TO THE FLOOR.  HE
SCRAMBLES AFTER THEM.  THE PHONE KEEPS RINGING.

                    IRVING

Will somebody get that phone.  (TO RUTH)

I can't find my tickets to "Chorus Line".

                    RUTH

How can I be expected to keep accurate

records with the adding machine screwed

up.  Your tickets to what!

                    IRVING

"A Chorus Line".  What's wrong with the

adding machine?  Is that going to be

another repair bill?  Business being what

it is, all you need is the subtract

key.  Isn't anyone going to answer the

phone?

                    RUTH

Just look at this mess... (REMEMBERING)

There's a phone message on your desk.

THE PHONE CONTINUES TO RING AS IRVING RUMMAGES THROUGH THE
DEBRIS ON HIS DESK IN SEARCH OF THE PHONE MESSAGE.

IRVING

Was it this message from the IRS?

Doesn't anyone _ever_ use the phone message

pad?  For God's sake, this is written on

the back of my "Chorus Line" tickets.

Harry, get the phone, will you.

RUTH

Harry's not here.  (LOOKING AT ADDING

MACHINE TAPE)  According to this, we

charged Paramount $75,000. for three

pages of revisions.

IRVING

Well, then why aren't we making any

money? I wonder what the IRS wants?

_IRVING_
_He's never here. Where is_
_he, at the dentist again?_

_HARRY GLIDES IN BUT IS UNNOTICED_
_BY IRVING AND RUTH._
_HARRY_
_I'm back. Why isn't anyone_
_answering the phone? I'm_
_going to lunch._
_HARRY EXITS._

RUTH

Tax on $72,000.00.  We have to buy a new

adding machine.  (PAUSE, REFERRING TO

PHONE)  I'll get that.  Hello, may we

help you?  (PAUSE, TO IRVING)  It's

Paramount.

IRVING

I don't know what keeps this place going.

RUTH

They have a question about a bill.

IRVING

I'm not in.  You handle it.

CUT TO:

C

INT. OFFICE - NEXT DAY
(Irving, Ruth)

RUTH IS IMMERSED IN A SPREADSHEET WHICH EXTENDS COMPLETELY
ACROSS HER DESK.  SHE ROLLS BACK AND FORTH IN HER CHAIR AS
THE VARIOUS ENTRIES DICTATE.  IRVING APPEARS IN THE DOORWAY.

                    IRVING

My wife is having an affair.  I just

found out... from the cleaning lady.

(THOUGHTFUL)  Come to think of it, I

wonder how she found out?

                    RUTH

The question is, why did she tell you.

Did I tell you the landlord is raising

the rent?

                    IRVING

I don't know why my wife would tell her

anyway... ~~they don't even like each~~

~~other...~~

The following blue revision pages
reflect changes, revised slugs and
asterisks.  These pages would be
distributed to production personnel
so that all existing scripts can be
updated and kept current.

                         RUTH

          Something's really wrong with this adding

          machine.  (RIPS OUT TAPE)  Look at

          this.  I added forty-seven plus three and

          came up with one hundred and five.  It's          *

          all screwed up.                                   *

SFX:  PHONE RINGS

IRVING ENTERS THE OFFICE IN A FLURRY, SITS AT HIS DESK AND
OPENS HIS BRIEFCASE.  SOME PAPERS FALL TO THE FLOOR.  HE
SCRAMBLES AFTER THEM.  THE PHONE KEEPS RINGING.

                        IRVING

          Will somebody get that phone.  (TO RUTH)

          I can't find my tickets to "Chorus Line".

                         RUTH

          How can I be expected to keep accurate

          records with the adding machine screwed

          up.  Your tickets to what!

                        IRVING

          "A Chorus Line".  What's wrong with the

          adding machine?  Is that going to be

          another repair bill?  Business being what

          it is, all you need is the subtract

          key.  Isn't anyone going to answer that

          phone?

                         RUTH

          Just look at this mess... (REMEMBERING)

          There's a phone message on your desk.

THE <u>PHONE CONTINUES TO RING</u> AS IRVING RUMMAGES THROUGH THE
DEBRIS ON HIS DESK IN SEARCH OF THE PHONE MESSAGE.

                         IRVING

          Was it this message from the IRS?

          Doesn't anyone <u>ever</u> use the phone message

          pad?  For God's sake this is written on

          the back of my "Chorus Line" tickets.

          Harry, get the phone, will you.

                         RUTH

          Harry's not here.

                         IRVING                               *

          He's <u>never</u> here.  Where is he, at the

          dentist again?

                         RUTH

          (LOOKING AT ADDING MACHINE TAPE)

          According to this, we charged Paramount

          $72,000 for three pages of revisions.

                         IRVING

          Well, then why aren't we making any

          money?

HARRY GLIDES IN, BUT IS UNNOTICED BY IRVING AND RUTH.          *

                         HARRY                                 *

          I'm back.  Why isn't anyone answering the

          phone?  I'm going to lunch.

HARRY EXITS.                                                   *

                         IRVING

          I wonder what the IRS wants.

                              RUTH

Tax on $72,000.00.  We have to buy a new

adding machine.  (PAUSE, REFERRING TO

PHONE)  I'll get that.  Hello, may we

help you?  (PAUSE, TO IRVING)  It's

Paramount.  They have a question about                              *

a bill.

                             IRVING

I'm not in.  You handle it.

                                             CUT TO:

C

INT. OFFICE - NEXT DAY
(Irving, Ruth)

RUTH IS IMMERSED IN A SPREADSHEET WHICH EXTENDS COMPLETELY
ACROSS HER DESK.  SHE ROLLS BACK AND FORTH IN HER CHAIR AS
THE VARIOUS ENTRIES DICTATE.  IRVING APPEARS IN THE DOORWAY.

                    IRVING

          My wife is having an affair.  I just

          found out... from the cleaning lady.

          (THOUGHTFUL)  Come to think of it, I

          wonder how she found out?

                    RUTH

          The question is, why did she tell you.

          Did I tell you the landlord is raising

          the rent?

                    IRVING

          I don't know why my wife would tell her

          anyway.                                              *

<u>GAME SHOWS</u>

Preliminaries

Game shows are in a category of their own.  While these shows are
scripted as are all other shows, the script serves more like a
"skeleton" of procedures since so many of the sequences are the same
from show to show.  The announcer, for example, opens and closes the
show the same way each time.  The M.C.'s explanation of the game
rules and various other parts of his dialogue is also the same from
show to show.  Aside from ad libs with the contestants and line
changes for prizes and/or money, these shows are predictably
formulated.

The format is quite different from other taped shows because a "two-
sided" format is used.  Essentially, it is an audio/visual format.
The AUDIO (all dialogue and sound) appears on the left half of the
page and the VIDEO (visuals) appears on the right half of the
page.  The format allows slightly more width for the audio on the
left side because the bulk of written material is here.

Format

    Tabs (11, 16, 21, 28, 61, 73)

    NAME OF THE SHOW - line 4, centered, capitalized, underlined
    PAGE NUMBER - line 4, tab (73)

    AUDIO - line 6, tab (21), capitalized, underlined
    VIDEO - line 6, tab (61), capitalized, underlined.

<u>Left Side</u>

        OPENING MUSIC THEME (or whatever), margin (11), double
    spaced down from AUDIO

        CHARACTER CUE - tab (28), capitalized, double spaced down
    from preceding.

        DIALOGUE - tab (16), double spaced down from character cue,
    upper/lower case, double spaced throughout.  Cut off at tab
    (36)

        APPLAUSE - Margin (11), capitalized, in parentheses.

<u>Right Side</u>

        <u>SET:</u> - double spaced down from "VIDEO", tab (51),
    capitalized, underlined, punctuated with a colon.  Items in
    the set are listed in a column under the first set listing.

        ALL OTHER VIDEO information appears at tab (51) across from
    the audio material to which it relates.

(MORE) and (CONT'D) are used in the conventional manner when
dialogue continues from one page to the next.

(See following example pages.)

"WORD WHIZ"

| AUDIO | VIDEO |
|---|---|

MUSIC:_ "WORD WHIZ" THEME

SET:  PODIUM FOR M.C.
      2 CONTESTANT DESKS
      2 OVERHEAD PROJECTOR
      SCREENS BEHIND DESKS

RAY (V.O.)

Welcome to "Word Whiz", the
game where contestants get a
chance to use their word power
to win money and prizes.  And
now, here's the star of "Word
Whiz", Monty Barker.

(APPLAUSE)                          MONTY ENTERS.

MONTY

Hello and welcome to all you
wizards of words to the show.
Words, words, words.  We all
use words every day but today
two contestants will use words
to compete for money and
prizes.  Here's how it works.


In round one we show the
contestants a five letter
word.  They then have thirty
seconds to write as many
different words as they can
using those five letters.

(MORE)

AUDIO                                                    VIDEO

MONTY (CONT'D)

At the end of the round, if the
same word is used by both
contestants, that word is
eliminated.  Whoever gets the
most words is awarded five
points.

In round two, the contestants
will be given a four letter
word.  But this time they will
compete verbally.  Taking
turns, each contestant will be
given five seconds to call out
a word using those four
letters.  If a contestant
cannot name a word in five
seconds, the other contestant
has the opportunity to call out
another word within five
seconds and so on.  At the end
of one minute, whoever calls
out the most words will be
awarded ten points.

(MORE)

| AUDIO | VIDEO |
|---|---|

The winning contestant will
receive $100.00 and will play
the Grand Slam Word Whiz round
and could become the next Word
Whiz champion and win $500.00,
an assortment of prizes, and --
a fabulous trip.  Ray, will you
tell us about those prizes
right now.

           RAY (V.O.)               PIC OF SPIEGEL CATALOGUE

A $100.00 gift certificate from
Spiegel Catalogue, where
shopping is at your fingertips.


A portable color TV set for          ZOYOTA LOGO
your car by the makers of
Zoyota -- who say, "Put a
little entertainment in your
back seat."  And...


From Disposable, a six month         PIC:  RAINBOW TRASH BAGS
supply of rainbow colored,
scented trash bags.  They're so
pretty, you hate to throw them
away.

| AUDIO | VIDEO |
|---|---|

### MONTY

Let's meet our contestants.

(MONTY INTRODUCES CONTESTANT
#1: _____)

BACK TO MONTY

SHOT OF CONTESTANT #1

SHOT OF CONTESTANT #2

(MONTY INTRODUCES CONTESTANT
#2: _____)

(MONTY AD LIBS WITH CONTESTANTS)

### MONTY

Okay.  We're ready to start

the first round.  Remember,

you have thirty seconds to

write as many words as you can

using this word:

And the word is:  _____.

5 LETTER WORD APPEARS ON
ELECTRONIC BOARD.

MUSIC: TBA

(CONTESTANTS BEGIN WRITING)

SHOTS OF CONTESTANTS,
AUDIENCE REACTION, SCREEN
BEHIND CONTESTANTS SHOWING
THE WORDS BEING WRITTEN.

### MONTY

Okay.  Time's up, contestants.

Let's see what you have.

(MONTY DETERMINES WHICH CONTESTANT
WINS FIRST ROUND AND RECEIVES FIVE
POINTS)

| AUDIO | VIDEO |
|---|---|

MONTY

Now we're ready for the second round.  In this round, contestants, you will call out your words and you have only five seconds apiece to call out your word.  At the end of one minute the contestant with the most words wins round two, and goes on to play the Grand Slam Word Whiz round.  The word for this round is _____.

4 LETTER WORD APPEARS ON ELECTRONIC BOARD.

(MONTY SIGNALS CONTESTANT #2 TO BEGIN)

SUPERIMPOSE TIME CLOCK TO SHOW TIME ELAPSING.

SFX:  BUZZER SOUNDS WHEN CONTESTANT HAS USED UP 5 SECONDS

MONTY

Time's up, contestants.

(MONTY DETERMINES WINNER)

# GLOSSARY

"A" PAGE        A term used to describe additional pages in a script in the revision process. The page number is used along with "A", "B", "C", etc., in order to keep the pages consecutive.

AD LIB        Extemporaneous lines or phrases appropriate to a given situation. There may, for example, be AD LIB greetings when guests arrive.

AUDIO/VIDEO        Sound and visuals. Used in a two-sided format found in game show scripts. The audio material appears on the left side of the page and the video (visuals) on the right side.

B.G.
(BACKGROUND)        Any activity in a scene that is secondary or subordinate to the main action and which serves as a backdrop for that action. Always abbreviated in capital letters (taped format), (lower case in film format), with periods after each letter. Appears only in direction.

BACKGROUND        Written out when referring to sounds in BACKGROUND of scene.

BARS        Pertains to orchestration or a single musical instrument. Numerals indicating the number of instrumental music bars to be played appear within the lyric. These numbers are stated: (-2-) or (-8-) or (-12-) GUITAR, for example.

CAMERA CUE        Specific direction given to the camera to achieve a desired effect. Examples: FOLLOW, PULL BACK, FIND, MOVE, ZOOM IN, CLOSE ON, etc.

CAST        A listing of the characters, including extras, appearing in a production. The list usually includes the names of the actors/actresses playing the various roles.

CAST CALL        A listing of times and places where each cast member must report for such things as make-up, wardrobe, etc. Usually appears on the cast page of each day's taping schedule.

CLOSE SHOT        A camera shot involving just the shoulders and head of a character. Similar but not to be confused with CLOSEUP. Always spelled out and capitalized. Underlined in tape format.

GLOSSARY

CLOSEUP             A camera shot that closely examines and/or
                    emphasizes some detail either on a person or an
                    inanimate object.   Always spelled out and
                    capitalized.  Underlined in tape format.

COLD OPENING        Indicates that a short segment opens the show
                    "cold" before the opening titles roll.  A term
                    used mainly in television variety shows.

COMBINATION PAGE    A page assigned two or more consecutive page
                    numbers to account for pages that have been
                    deleted from the script as a result of
                    revision.  Page numbers are stated:  11/12 or
                    85-87.

CONTACT LIST        A listing of the names, addresses, and phone
                    numbers of all the personnel involved with a
                    specific television production.   The contact
                    list is used mainly in variety, award, and
                    special shows.

CONTINUOUS          Used to indicate that there has been no time
ACTION              lapse in the action when we come back to a
                    given scene even though another scene or scenes
                    or possibly a commercial may have intervened.

DISSOLVE            A scene ending used to indicate that the scene
                    should gradually fade away.

DOLLY               A camera cue used in direction instructing the
                    camera to move along with the subjects of the
                    scene.  This is achieved by either a hand-held
                    camera or a camera secured to an apparatus on
                    wheels.  Always capitalized.  Rarely used in
                    taped formats.

EDITING             Deleting or re-arranging material.  This takes
                    place after a production has been video taped
                    or filmed.  Video tape also allows for "on the
                    spot editing."   When "editing" occurs in
                    scripts, it is referred to as revision.

ELLIPSES            A series of three periods used to signify a
                    pause or a change in thought sequence. Use of
                    the ellipsis may indicate that a word or words
                    are left out because they are "understood".

ESU                 Engineering setup.

## GLOSSARY

**EXT. (EXTERIOR)**  Indicates that a scene will be shot at an outdoor location. In taped shows, a set in the studio may be made to look like it is outside. Used in scene headings or set headings, it is always abbreviated in capital letters, punctuated with a period.

**EXTREME CLOSEUP (ECU)**  The camera is in very close, usually on an object, for purposes of spotlighting a detail. Sometimes incorrectly written ECU but correctly must appear spelled out in capital letters. Underlined in taped formats.

**FADE IN:**  To bring in the first scene of an act (or the beginning of a feature). Always spelled out, capitalized, punctuated with a colon. Underlined in tape formats.

**FADE OUT.**  An act ending used at the end of an act and at the end of the script. Scene gradually darkens to black. Spelled out, capitalized, punctuated with a period. Underlined in taped formats.

**FILM FORMAT**  The specific script format used for a "one camera" production. Distinguished from taped television format because of the technique of shooting partly on location. Interchangeably used with screenplay, one camera, and feature film format.

**F.G. (FOREGROUND)**  Those activities which take place nearest the viewer in perspective. Opposite of B.G. Always abbreviated in capital letters (taped format), (lower case in film format), with periods after each letter.

**FLY PAGE**  (Also title page.) The first page appearing after the cover in most filmed or taped scripts. Basic material here is title of the show or film, episode title (series shows), author's name, name and address of production company, producer, director, and sometimes other production personnel (taped shows), draft, date, etc.

**FREEZE FRAME.**  A camera technique wherein the action is stopped becoming a still photograph. Works as a camera cue but isolated at the margin. Punctuated by a period.

## GLOSSARY

"FRONT" PAGES      Pages of "special", specific information appearing just before the body of the script in taped shows. Includes: Contact Lists (Staff, Crew, Cast), Schedules (Rehearsal, Taping, Blocking), Short Rundown (SRD).

"HOLD"      To keep the same. Applies to scene and page numbers in revisions. All page and scene numbers must be accounted for by using "A" scenes or pages or using combination numbers to accommodate additional or ommited information.

IN PRODUCTION      All preliminary work has been completed and a show is currently being filmed or taped.

INT. (INTERIOR)      Indicates that a particular scene will be shot inside. Used in scene headings, abbreviated in capital letters, using a period.

INTO:      Appears at the bottom of the script page to indicate what comes next: a specific musical number, segment, award, etc., in variety, award, and special shows. Capitalized, punctuated with a colon. This information is usually in parenthesis.

LEFT HANDED FORMAT      Tape-Live format normally appearing on left side of page is positioned on the right side of page to accommodate left handed directors. In this way, notes can more easily be written on left side of the page.

LIMBO SET      A small, unidentifiable portion of larger set used in close or medium shot revealing character engaged in isolated activity such as talking on pay phone. Background details not necessary.

LIVE      Refers to shows taped before a live audience. Television shows rarely broadcast live in the sense that the audience sees it at the moment it occurs. Exceptions are such events as The Rose Parade and the Academy Awards.

LRD (LONG RUNDOWN)      Listing of show segments, musical numbers and script page numbers characterized by large spaces on page on which technicians write notes.

MOVING OR MOVING SHOT      A camera cue used in direction to indicate that the camera should move with whatever moving object or person being filmed.

## GLOSSARY

O.C.
(OFF CAMERA)
Sounds or dialogue heard while the camera is on another subject.  Means the same as off screen (O.S.); however, OFF CAMERA is the term used in taped television formats. Stated: (O.C.) next to the character cue and O.C. in direction.

O.S.
(OFF SCREEN)
Same as O.C. (off camera).  O.S. is correct term used in a film show. Example: a character talking or calling from another room.  Stated (O.S.) next to the character cue and O.S. in direction.

PAN (PANNING)
Camera moves slowly from left to right or vice versa, not stopping on any one thing or person.  Spelled out in capital letters. Rarely used in taped format.

PLAYON or
PLAYOFF
A few musical bars used to introduce a performer to "play him/her on" stage. Conversely, PLAYOFF indicates musical bars used for exit.  Used in variety, award, and special shows.

POST PRODUCTION
Those parts of the production that are facilitated after the major shooting has been completed.  Sound effects, music background, music "sweetening," stock footage, etc., are handled at this time. Applies mainly to film.

PROPS
Those special items required in a specific scene or segment of a show.  Props include such things as a "diamond ring", a picnic basket, food items, etc.

PRE-PRODUCTION
Those parts of the production that are prepared before filming or taping a show.  Meetings are held with the show personnel and necessary preparations are made.

REHEARSAL
SCHEDULE
Schedule of times and places where performers and technical crew must appear for the rehearsing and blocking of a taped television show.

REVISION PAGES
Pages or portions of pages that have been changed or material added.  Revised pages are used when a film or taped show is in production.  The pages are color-coded to flag changes that have occurred.

RUN
Several revision pages in consecutive sequence.

SCENE
A continuous sequence or package of action.

## GLOSSARY

| | |
|---|---|
| SEGMENT | Comedy skit, musical number, award presentation, etc. Variety, award, and special shows are broken up in segments. |
| SEGMENT CAST | The cast of performers in a particular skit, musical number, award presentation, etc. The cast names are listed on the first page of the segment directly under the segment slug. |
| SET | Refers to a specific (usually interior) place such as a living room, a restaurant, etc. Used in taped shows. |
| SFX: (SOUND EFFECTS) | Sound effects which requiring technical reproduction. The wind blowing is a sound effect. Written SFX: and isolated at the margin. Used in tape formats. |
| SHOT | A camera angle or instruction such as CLOSE SHOT, EXTREME CLOSEUP, LONG SHOT, etc. |
| SIMULTANEOUS DIALOGUE | Two characters speaking at the same time. Dialogue is often written side by side on the page. Margins must be re-set to accommodate this situation. |
| SIMULTANEOUS LYRICS | Two sets of song lyrics sung at the same time. While the main lyric is sung, a chorus may back it up with ooohh's and ahhh's or possibly with repeated lines of lyric. Simultaneous lyrics appear side by side on the page. |
| SITCOM | A shortened term meaning situation comedy. Traditionally half-hour television shows wherein sterotyped characters are involved in an ongoing set in various situations. |
| SKETCH | Comedy segments or skits in variety or special shows. Essentially short sitcoms with sterotyped characters using a situational vehicle. |
| SLUG | Heading information. May be a segment slug in a variety, award, or special show, a set slug in a sitcom or a scene slug in a filmed show. |
| SOUND CUES | Indication that a particular sound or sounds are called for. It may be a sound indicated in direction or a sound effect isolated at the margin (in taped shows). |
| SOUND CUES (GENERALIZED) | General background sounds that will be heard throughout a scene or sequence. Rain is one. |

## GLOSSARY

SPFX:
(SPECIAL
EFFECTS)

Special effects requiring technical reproduction. Smoke billowing from under a door is one. Stated SPFX:, isolated at the margin. Used in tape show formats.

SRD
(SHORT RUNDOWN)

Basically serves as timing sheets and a kind of table of contents listing the scenes or segments (including musical numbers) in the show. The cast is also listed along with the script page number references. Boxes are provided to record timings.

STAGE DIRECTION

Sometimes called the "business." Describes the fabric or fiction of the scene: the mood, the situation, the characters, general character instructions, camera and sound cues, notes to the director, etc. Any information needed to facilitate the scene. It is the "business" of the scene.

STOCK

Film footage already shot kept on "file" in the film archives. Used in scenes frequently re-establishing a location continually re-occuring or enhancing a film with shots that would normally be expensive and difficult to capture. Footage of World War I planes flying is an example. A coiled rattlesnake is the most common use of a stock shot. Sometimes used in taped shows, as well.

SUPER
(SUPERIMPOSE)

The effect of showing one thing over another in the same shot. Titles and/or credits are often "supered" over the beginning or ending sequences of a film.

TABS

Typewriter stops set at various intervals across the page. Necessary for the positioning of dialogue, scene endings, etc.

TAG

A short "wrap up" scene at the end of a taped television show. Usually less than two pages.

TAPED FORMAT

The specific script format used for a taped television production. Two different formats are used, both of which differ greatly from filmed format. Sometimes called television format.

TAPING (VIDEO)

Recording or "shooting" on video tape using television cameras. A very different technique than filming a show with a movie camera.

TAPING SCHEDULE

A schedule set up for the video taping of a television show.

## GLOSSARY

| | |
|---|---|
| TBA | To be announced. |
| THREE-CAMERA | Refers to video taping technique using basically three (but usually four or more) television cameras strategically placed for close shots, medium shots, moving shots, etc. |
| TRACK | A strip of magnetic tape on which sound is recorded on film or video tape. Dialogue is recorded during the actual shooting but other sounds such as music, sound effects, or laughter is recorded later. |
| VARIETY SHOW | A show incorporating various kinds of entertainment such as music, dance, comedy skits, etc. The basic format is Tape-Live. |
| VOICE OVER (V.O.) | Indicates the mechanical transmission of a character's voice heard over an instrument (telephone or tape recorder). Capitalized and abbreviated in parentheses next to the character cue. In tape format direction, written out, capitalized, and underlined. |
| VTPB: (VIDEO TAPE PLAY BACK) | Indicates that certain segments of a show were pre-recorded and will be played back at the appropriate time. "That's Incredible" and "Real People" use this technique. |
| ZOOM | The camera moves quickly forward in on a person or object. Capitalized and underlined in taped format but infrequently used in tape shows. |

FOLLOWING:  An Appendix for Quick Reference

## APPENDIX A

## TAB SETTINGS

### TAPE-LIVE FORMAT

(11, 16, 31, 73)

### Cutoffs

```
direction ......................... 41
personal direction ............... same as direction
dialogue .......................... 46
```

### THREE-CAMERA FORMAT

(11, 21, 36, 61, 73)

### Cutoffs

```
direction ......................... 76
personal direction................. 61
dialogue .......................... 61
```

### VARIETY SHOWS

(11, 16, 31, 73)

### Cutoffs

Same as Tape-Live Format

### SCHEDULES

(7, 26, 31, 61, 73)

### SHORT RUNDOWN (SRD)

(7, 12, 38, 73)

### LONG RUNDOWN (LRD)

(11, 16, [56], 69, 73)

## UNIVERSAL TRUTHS

The following is a collection of rules that consistently apply throughout all script formats.  Some correspond with grammatical rules and some with typing rules.  They are, in the long run, devised to promote clarity and consistency in all script formats.

GENERAL

1) Do not break a sentence from one page to another.  The sentence must be completed before going to the next page.

2) Always leave two spaces after the punctuation at the end of a sentence.

3) When using the ellipsis (three periods) to indicate a pause within a sentence, a space must be left after the last dot.

4) Dashes or hyphens may be used to indicate a pause in the same way in which the ellipsis is used.  Two dashes are used with a space on each side.

5) The word "okay" is always spelled out.

DIALOGUE  (When in doubt, spell it out)

1) Spell out all two digit numbers.  (Three digit numbers may be written numerically.)

2) Spell out indications of time.  Example:  one-thirty.

3) Spell out all personal titles except:  Mr., Mrs., and Ms.

4) Never hyphenate a word from one line to the next unless the word is normally hyphenated anyway.  Example:  son-in-law.

DIRECTION

1) Personal titles may be abbreviated.  (Sgt., Capt.)

2) Words may be hyphenated from one line to the next but this practice should be avoided whenever possible.

<u>APPENDIX C</u>

<u>(MORE) and (CONT'D)</u>

(MORE) is used only when dialogue continues onto the next page. Double space down from the last line of dialogue and state (MORE) on the same tab as the character cue.  Tape-Live Format is tab (31).  Three-Camera Format is tab (36).

(CONT'D) is used when a character's dialogue continues onto the next page and also when dialogue is interrupted by stage direction or optionally when dialogue is interrupted by the same character's personal direction (Tape-Live Format).

<u>EXAMPLE</u>

                CHARACTER

        Dialogue dialogue dialogue.

                (MORE)


-------------------------- next page ---------------------------


                CHARACTER (CONT'D)

        Dialogue dialogue dialogue...

STAGE DIRECTION STAGE DIRECTION
STAGE DIRECTION STAGE DIRECTION

                CHARACTER (CONT'D)

        Dialogue dialogue dialogue...

## ABBREVIATION, CAPITALIZATION AND PUNCTUATION

(Applies to both Tape-Live and Three-Camera formats unless otherwise indicated.)


## SET HEADINGS

### Abbreviations

1)    INT.
2)    EXT.

### Capitalization

All words

### Punctuation

1)    dashes used to separate elements
2)    parentheses used to enclose specific time
      indications such as (2:00)


## STAGE DIRECTION

### Abbreviations

1)    personal titles
2)    other standard abbreviations
3)    B.G.   (BACKGROUND)
4)    F.G.   (FOREGROUND)
5)    O.C.   (OFF CAMERA)

### Spell Out:

1)    VOICE OVER
2)    AD LIB

### Capitalization

All words

### Punctuation

1)    standard punctuation throughout
2)    in Tape-Live Format, enclosed in parentheses

### Underlining

1)    generalized sound cues
2)    camera cues
3)    AD LIB
4     VOICE OVER

## CHARACTER CUE

### Abbreviations

1)    personal titles
2)    (V.O.)
3)    (O.C.)

### Capitalization

All words

### Punctuation

parentheses around:

a)    (V.O.)
b)    (O.C.)
c)    (CONT'D)
d)    specific role designation after character name

## PERSONAL DIRECTION

### Abbreviations

Personal titles

### Capitalization

All words

### Punctuation

1)    Standard punctuation
2)    Enclosed in parentheses (both formats)

## DIALOGUE

### Abbreviations; only

1)    Mr.
2)    Mrs.
3)    Ms.

### Spell out

All other words including:
1)    one and two digit numbers
2)    personal titles
3)    time indications
4)    okay

DIALOGUE (CONT'D)

Punctuation

Standard punctuation or as per author
1)   a space left after the ellipsis (three periods)
2)   a space on each side of two dashes indicating pause


SCENE ENDINGS

Abbreviations

None

Capitalization

All words

Punctuation

Colon after all except FADE OUT., which is followed by a
period.